Homicide

on the

Isle of Man

Homicide
on the
Isle of Man

JOHN J. EDDLESTON

ROBERT HALE · LONDON

© *John J. Eddleston 2009*
First published in Great Britain 2009

ISBN 978-0-7090-8602-4

Robert Hale Limited
Clerkenwell House
Clerkenwell Green
London EC1R 0HT

www.halebooks.com

The right of John J. Eddleston to be identified as
author of this work has been asserted by him
in accordance with the Copyright, Designs
and Patents Act 1988

A catalogue record for this book is available from the British Library

2 4 6 8 10 9 7 5 3 1

Typeset by e-type, Liverpool
Printed in China and arranged by
New Era Printing Co. Ltd, Hong Kong

Contents

Acknowledgements

There are four people I wish to thank for their help in preparing this volume. First and foremost, I wish to thank my wife, Yvonne. She helped me research all of the cases from the mid-nineteenth century onwards, proof-read the entire volume, and suggested various improvements throughout. There is no way I would have finished the book on time, but for her assistance. I wish to thank Hampton Creer, the author of *Never to Return*, for his invaluable aid with the earlier cases.

I would also like to offer my sincere thanks to John Cowan LRPS who took some of the photographs in this book, and also Jason Roberts of Manx Radio for his assistance with a couple of the illustrations.

Note

This book covers every death sentence, murder case and manslaughter trial on the Isle of Man since the eighteenth century. Although the most common understanding of the term 'homicide' is just 'murder', in this book it is used more broadly to mean 'the action by a human being of killing a human being.' That is why two chapters detailing all the death sentences issued on the island are included, so that the work may be looked upon as definitive. No other book has conducted such a comprehensive survey of homicide on the Isle of Man before.

1

The Eighteenth Century

The Isle of Man authorities seldom handed out the penalty of death for crimes committed on the island and, even when such sentences were given, they were very rarely carried out. During the entire period of the eighteenth century, just twenty death sentences were given on the island and, of those, only nine executions actually took place.

The details of all these death sentences are given below.

Mary Taggart

In October 1717, Mary was convicted of causing the death of her illegitimate child and was duly sentenced to death. Soon afterwards, the Earl of Derby wrote to the island's governor asking that the sentence be carried out swiftly: '... Nevertheless, if the said Mary Taggart should rather choose to be transported to some of the foreign plantations belonging to His Majesty of Great Britain, you are to take the first opportunity to send her away ...' Mary did indeed take advantage of the opportunity and was transported abroad in February of the following year.

Robert Wilson and John Quick

Robert Wilson appeared in court in May 1724 and was found guilty of treason as a result of bringing into the island some counterfeit coinage, including sixteen half-crowns and six shillings. Sentenced to death, there was no reprieve or commutation of the sentence, and on 17 July he was hanged alongside John Quick, a petty thief.

John Kewley

Kewley was a native of Ballaugh and appears to have been arrested for theft – or at least the suspicion of theft. He was finally accused of stealing 20 pounds of pork, to the monetary value of four shillings, the property of William Craine of Braddan. He was further accused of stealing a rope and a sack, valued at eleven pence, from Gilnow Quine, also of Braddan.

Found guilty and sentenced to death, the execution was set for Friday, 16 June 1732, but Kewley too was offered the alternative of transportation, this time to Ireland on the condition that he joined the King's army, an offer he readily took up.

John Clucas, William Clucas and William Kelly

Brothers John and William Clucas were convicted of breaking into a house at Kirk Michael and stealing £34, a golden guinea and a silver spoon. William Kelly was accused of being their confederate and all three men were duly sentenced to death. On 8 August 1735, the three were hanged together at Castle Rushen.

In fact, although no violence occurred during the robbery itself, the affair did lead to the death of one other person. Kelly's father, John, was so devastated by what his son had done, and the consequences of that crime, that he tied his legs together and threw himself into a nearby river where he drowned.

William Cannell

Cannell lived in Patrick and admitted stealing 18 yards of material from Sylvester Fairbrother of Peel. Sentenced to

CASTLE RUSHEN CASTLE TOWN I.O.M.

Castle Rushen where prisoners were held on the Isle of Man

death, he appealed to the Duke of Atholl who commuted that sentence to one of transportation for life. Cannell left the island for an unknown destination on 7 August 1740.

Oates Cretney and William Kelly

Cretney and Kelly were being held in Castle Rushen to await trial for various felonious acts when, on 5 February 1741, Cretney escaped, probably the first man to achieve this feat. The governor of the island immediately signed orders stating that if the escaped prisoner did not hand himself in, he would be treated as an outlaw and death warrants would be issued against him. Cretney did not hand himself in and, consequently, the warrants were signed on 23 October of that year.

Kelly, who was Cretney's accomplice, appeared in court and was sentenced to death, but he too accepted the offer of transportation for life when it was offered.

Thomas Corraige

Corraige lived in Lezayre and in May 1741 stole a sheep and some wool. Sent for trial, he was adjudged to be guilty and sentenced to death, his execution being fixed for 22 May. The prisoner then petitioned the Duke of Atholl requesting that his sentence be commuted to one of voluntary transportation for life. This plea was granted in July of that same year.

John Bridson

John lived in Ballasalla with his wife, Elinor Bridson, née Taylor, and was found guilty of murdering her at his trial on 12 November 1745. Sentenced to death, various attempts were made to obtain mercy for him, but after a number of postponements he was finally hanged on 30 January 1746.

John Corlett

Corlett (or Curlett) was a shopkeeper in Castletown and on 2 May 1764 he battered his wife, Catherine, to death. Found guilty of murder on 9 October, he was originally due to hang on 19 October, but a number of postponements followed. Eventually the sentence was confirmed and Corlett was hanged on Friday, 22 February 1765.

Corlett left behind two children, now made orphans by the loss of their father and mother. By law, all of Corlett's possessions now fell into the hands of the Attorney General on behalf of the Lord and Lady of the Isle. A petition was made to request that the goods and possessions be returned to the two children and this was granted in December 1765.

Patrick Cottier

In 1765, Cottier was found guilty of robbery and sentenced to death. He petitioned that his sentence be commuted to one of voluntary transportation, or possibly employment in some business that might allow him to provide support for his family which included six children.

Cottier's appeal was successful, but he was then shocked to discover that his sentence would only be commuted on condition that he became the common executioner for the period of his natural life and would need to enter into a £50 bond and obligation for that purpose. Cottier agreed to the condition and signed an acceptance on 18 December 1765.

Soon afterwards, Cottier wrote to the governor, John Wood, stating that he could not raise the £50, and asking whether any other penalty could be laid upon him – including whipping or transportation. This plea fell on deaf ears and Cottier was confirmed in his new position as executioner for the island.

John Teare

A native of Maughold, convicted of sheep stealing and sentenced to death in 1770, Teare found himself in exactly the same predicament as the previous entry, Cottier, and was also appointed as common executioner.

Matthew Tracy and James Gallagher

On 16 January 1781, five Irishmen on horseback attacked Joseph Mortimer close to Governor's Bridge at Onchan. Mortimer was known to be a wealthy man and, since he was also elderly, his assailants must have believed he would be an easy target.

Mortimer was pulled from his own horse and assaulted before being robbed of forty-eight guineas, some silver coins, and his watch which was valued at £2.

Unfortunately for the attackers, the entire affair was witnessed by a local man who heard one of the miscreants being referred to as Tracy. Further, the witness was able to say that the five were members of a private militia, the Manx Fencibles.

Gatehouse of Castle Rushen

It was now a simple matter to find all five and, in due course, Matthew Tracy, James Gallagher, James Chapman, John Clark and Roger McGongill were arrested and charged. The five were placed on trial, but the latter three were acquitted. Tracy was convicted as his name had been uttered during the robbery and Gallagher's trousers were still stained with blood.

On 10 April 1781, Mr Dawson, the governor of the island, wrote to the jailer of Castle Rushen ordering that the subject of the previous entry, John Teare, be held in the castle as it was his duty under his agreement of 1770 to perform the execution of the two prisoners. Soon afterwards, Tracy and Gallagher were duly hanged.

William Watterson and Thomas Watterson

In September 1783, William Watterson broke into a house at Castletown that was owned by John Quayle and John Taubman. William Watterson was seen smashing a window in order to gain access and then using a crowbar to force open a desk. In all, Watterson stole twenty-three guineas in gold, silver and copper coinage.

Arrested and charged, William Watterson escaped from prison and fled to Ireland. There he was eventually recognized and brought back to the Isle of Man where he faced his trial in March 1786.

Towards the end of January in that same year, Thomas Watterson stole a piece of olive-coloured calico, valued at £3, from a Castletown shop belonging to Edward Gelling. He too was arrested and both brothers appeared in court together.

The Wattersons were sentenced to death, but this was subsequently commuted to transportation. They arrived in Liverpool together on 12 August, from where they escaped. Recaptured, they were sent on to London and then, finally, on to Honduras.

John Callister

Callister was a blacksmith from Ramsey who stole 500 salted herrings from Robert Christian of Maughold. At the time, he was accompanied by his father, David, who apparently was the instigator of the crime and had led John into trouble.

David Callister fled the island soon after the crime, but John was arrested and charged, appearing in court in July 1787. Found guilty and sentenced to death, on the 28th of the same month, John appealed – stating that he had been influenced by his father and agreeing to be transported. The appeal was successful and John left the island soon afterwards, for an unknown destination.

Summary

Name	Year	Crime	Final sentence
Mary Taggart	1717	Murder	Transported
Robert Wilson	1724	Treason (Counterfeiting)	Executed
John Quick	1724	Theft	Executed
John Kewley	1732	Suspicion of theft	Transported
John Clucas	1735	Burglary	Executed
William Clucas	1735	Burglary	Executed
William Kelly	1735	Confederacy	Executed
William Cannell	1740	Theft	Transported
Oates Cretney	1741	Felony	Escaped
William Kelly	1741	Felony	Transported
Thomas Corraige	1741	Sheep stealing	Transported
John Bridson	1746	Murder	Executed
John Corlett	1765	Murder	Executed
Patrick Cottier	1765	Robbery	Became hangman
John Teare	1770	Sheep stealing	Became hangman
Matthew Tracy	1781	Highway robbery	Executed
James Gallagher	1781	Highway robbery	Executed
William Watterson	1786	Burglary	Transported
Thomas Watterson	1786	Burglary	Transported
John Callister	1787	Theft	Transported

2

The Early Nineteenth Century (1800–50)

We have seen that there were nine executions in the eighteenth century, but such events became even rarer over the following 100 years. In the first half of the new century, just six executions were carried out and only one more, the seventh and final one to be carried out on the island, took place after 1850. This chapter tells the stories behind the crimes that earned a sentence of death by hanging from 1800 to 1850.

Robert Quilliam – 1816

Robert was found guilty of sheep stealing and duly sentenced to death. He petitioned that he might be transported instead and was eventually sent to New South Wales.

Robert Kewley – 1818

Kewley was also found guilty of sheep stealing and sentenced to death, but for him there was to be no escape from the noose.

It was in this year that a new gallows was erected at the top end of Castletown harbour and this was where Kewley was executed on Friday, 27 May 1818. It was the first hanging of the nineteenth century.

Richard Humphrey Templeton – 1820

Sentenced to death for rape, Templeton's sentence was commuted to one of transportation and he was sent to New South Wales in September 1821.

Philip Fargher – 1823

Fargher was convicted of sheep stealing in March 1823 and sentenced to hang. However, the Duke of Atholl himself intervened and wrote to the authorities in Whitehall stating that he did not believe that the trial had been conducted properly. Further, he said, it was unsafe to execute a man where there was such doubt and the letter added a recommendation that the prisoner should be transported instead. Fargher was indeed transported, to Tasmania, in August of that same year.

John Carnaish and Catherine Kinrade – 1823

John and Catherine were lovers and she soon became pregnant. There was, however, a problem in the fact that John was a married man. The solution appeared to be simple; the wife had to be disposed of and was duly poisoned by means of arsenic added to her porridge.

The two miscreants were put on trial, found guilty, and sentenced to death. While in prison, Catherine gave birth to a healthy child, but it did nothing to save her from the gallows and the pair were hanged together on 18 April 1823. The execution, though, was not without incident. In deference to her sex, the rope was not placed tightly around Catherine's neck, so that when the cart was driven away it was seen that her toes touched the ground. The newspaper reports of the day claimed that this did not prolong her agony. Afterwards, both bodies were given over to the surgeons for dissection: Carnaish in Douglas and Kinrade in

Ramsey. As for Catherine's child, it was taken off the island and into care so that it would never know the ignominy of its parents' demise.

William Kelly – 1824

At this time, burglary was a capital offence. Kelly was found guilty of smashing a window, getting in the house, and stealing three half-crowns and a further eighteen shillings in cash, a total of twenty-five shillings and six pence. He was sentenced to hang by Deemsters Christian and Heywood, but what may surprise the reader is that Kelly was only twelve years old.

Details of the death sentence were passed on to London for approval, but fortunately the Secretary of State substituted a sentence of transportation for life.

In 1825, by which time he had reached the age of thirteen, Kelly was sent to Tasmania.

Anne Garrett – 1827

Anne stole a sheep from a neighbour, William Garrett, and was in the process of butchering the animal, assisted by her husband and son, when the local constable came upon the scene. It was then that Anne compounded her crime by offering the officer a cow if he would turn a blind eye.

Anne Garrett appeared before Deemster Heywood, was found guilty, and sentenced to death by hanging. An appeal was entered and succeeded, with the sentence being reduced to one of transportation. She travelled to Tasmania with the youngest of her six children, but was released from the sentence in 1839.

Robert Morrison – 1827

In 1827 an argument broke out between Morrison and one Daniel Quiggin who had, apparently, made insulting remarks about Morrison's manhood. The argument then escalated to the point where Morrison drew out a knife and fatally stabbed Quiggin in the side.

Sentenced to death for murder, the sentence was commuted by the British authorities and Morrison was transported instead.

John Bailey Lyons – 1828

Lyons was accused of bringing counterfeit currency into the island. He was found guilty and sentenced to death by Deemster Christian. However, since this was technically also a crime of treason, there was to be the added refinement that, after hanging, Lyons's head was to be struck off.

The sentence was not carried out for Lyons was granted mercy and received fourteen years' transportation instead. He was sent on to New South Wales where he died in 1874.

Thomas Kerruish – 1829

A convicted rapist, Kerruish was hanged at Castle Rushen on 19 June 1829, on what was his twenty-fifth birthday. It is reported that his death was a difficult one and that he struggled at the end of the rope for some minutes.

Mary Millan – 1831

Another prisoner convicted of sheep stealing, Mary had slaughtered the animal and was carrying the carcass back to her home in a sack. The burden proved to be somewhat heavy and she sat down to take a breather. Two men came up to her and she asked them for help in carrying the bundle; unfortunately for Mary, the two men were employees of Captain Moses from whom she had stolen the sheep.

Mary was found guilty and sentenced to death, but that

sentence was commuted to one of transportation. She left the Isle of Man for Australia in August 1831.

John McGhee – 1832

McGhee was found guilty of sheep stealing and sentenced to death, but eventually the Secretary of State intervened and McGhee was transported instead. He left the island in August 1832, one year after Mary Millan.

Thomas Siddleton and James Moore – 1832

Siddleton and Moore attacked William Kinley, an advocate, at Peel. Kinley was very badly beaten, but made a full receevery from his injuries – and also named the two attackers who had also stolen his purse containing almost £40.

Moore readily admitted that he was one of the two men responsible, but Siddleton claimed he knew nothing of the crime. But this denial did nothing to save him, and both men were found guilty and sentenced to death. They were hanged together, at Castle Rushen, on 22 October.

William Roxburgh – 1838

Roxburgh broke into a house in Ramsey, owned by one William Radcliff, and stole a number of items including two balls of wool and two pairs of shoes. His nephew, William Gordon, who was just fifteen, helped him in this crime. When the boy was arrested, he told officials the whole story. Roxburgh was arrested and, after being found guilty, was sentenced to death. Once again, mercy was granted and William was transported.

William Moore – 1841

Moore broke into a house in Douglas in November 1841, but

was discovered by the occupant, Hugh Bridson, who attacked Moore and rendered him unconscious.

Put on trial before Deemster Heywood and sentenced to death, Moore had that sentence reduced to one of transportation by the Secretary of State in London.

Thomas Cowley – 1844

Thomas Cowley was sentenced to death for the murder of his wife. He had thrown a stone at her head that struck and killed her. After the sentence was given, Cowley was found to be of unsound mind and was ordered to be held until His Majesty's pleasure be known.

Robert Radcliffe – 1846

Radcliffe broke into a house at Lezayre and stole a watch, for which crime he was sentenced to hang. He appealed against the sentence and was finally transported to Tasmania instead. He never returned to the island, dying at Hobart in 1852.

Richard Roberts – 1850

In January 1850, Roberts broke into the post office in Thomas Street in Douglas, but once inside he encountered the postmistress, Eleanor Macadam, who chased him from the premises and eventually captured him in Factory Lane. He tried desperately to escape, but fortunately for Eleanor her brother, Noble, came to her aid.

Arrested and tried before Deemster Heywood, Roberts was sentenced to death. The sentence was then commuted to one of imprisonment, which he served at the Millbank prison, situated close to Vauxhall Bridge in London.

Summary

Name	Year	Crime	Final Sentence
Robert Quilliam	1816	Sheep stealing	Transported
Robert Kewley	1818	Sheep stealing	Executed
Richard Templeton	1820	Rape	Transported
Philip Fargher	1823	Sheep stealing	Transported
John Carnaish	1823	Murder	Executed
Catherine Kinrade	1823	Murder	Executed
William Kelly	1824	Burglary	Transported
Anne Garrett	1827	Sheep stealing	Transported
Robert Morrison	1827	Murder	Transported
John Bailey	1828	Forgery	Transported
Thomas Kerruish	1829	Rape	Executed
Mary Millan	1831	Sheep stealing	Transported
John McGee	1832	Sheep stealing	Transported
Thomas Siddleton	1832	Attempted murder	Executed
James Moore	1832	Attempted murder	Executed
William Roxburgh	1838	Burglary	Transported
William Moore	1841	Burglary	Transported
Thomas Cowley	1844	Murder	Unsound mind
Robert Radcliffe	1846	Burglary	Transported
Richard Roberts	1850	Burglary	Imprisonment

3

The Postman

Thomas Corrin was puzzled. Late on the evening of Tuesday, 16 January 1866, he was travelling along the road between Castletown and Ballasalla when he found a horse-driven cart without a driver.

Corrin could see that the cart was in fact the mail gig from Douglas and the foot-board appeared to be damaged on the left-hand side. He waited for around fifteen minutes, to see if the missing driver would appear but, when he didn't, Corrin did his duty and took the cart into Castletown where he delivered it to the post office.

An immediate search was made for John Kermode, the missing driver, but no trace of him could be found along the track or in the woods around Ballasalla – though it was confirmed that he had delivered one bag of mail at the post office there.

In 1866, the system was that mail would arrive from England on the boats from Liverpool and be taken to the post office in Athol Street, Douglas. Under normal circumstances, this meant that the mail for Castletown would leave the capital some time after 5 p.m., but on 16 January the boat had been delayed and did not arrive in Douglas until 8.30 p.m. The local island mail had already been taken, but such was the postal service at this time that a second delivery would now have to be made, no matter what the time. Kermode had been detailed to take the mail and had three stops on his journey. First, he would call at the post office at Kirk Stanton, then go on to Ballasalla, and finally go to Castletown. He had indeed made

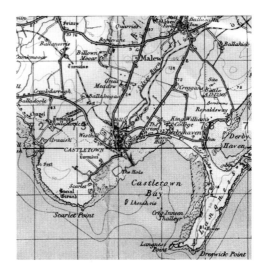

The area where John Kermode was killed

the first two deliveries, but had never completed the twelve-minute or so journey from Ballasalla to Castletown.

On the afternoon of Wednesday, 17 January, at around 3 p.m., the same Thomas Corrin who had found the mail gig the previous evening was trimming some twigs along the river bank some half a mile from Castletown when he found the body of the missing man. Kermode lay face down in a shallow stream, on the west side, close to the bank; he was obviously dead. Corrin wasted no time in reporting his discovery.

The inquest on John Kermode opened on Friday, 19 June, at Castletown, before the coroner general for inquests, William Christian. Evidence of identification was given, after which John Jones was called to give medical evidence. He testified that Kermode had died as a result of drowning and, after this, the body was released to Matthias Caine, a brother-in-law of the dead man.

It was around 2.30 p.m. when Caine arrived to collect Kermode's body, and noticed that the man was fully dressed with his coat still buttoned up and his cap tied on. In the process of preparing the body for removal, Caine noticed that there was some blood on John Kermode's cap and, upon removing it, he found a wound on the back of the head. Caine sent for the doctor who arrived within fifteen minutes.

Caine pointed out the wound to Dr Jones and noticed he looked rather surprised. At one stage he put a finger into the wound and announced that it was merely a scratch. Matthias Caine, though, was far from satisfied and reported his finding to the authorities. As a result, the highly unusual step was taken of ordering a second inquest and this opened on Saturday, 20 January, before the same coroner who had presided over the first inquest.

The first witness was John Kerruish who, like Kermode, was a letter-carrier. He confirmed that he had known the deceased for a number of years and it had been he who handed three bags of mail over to Kermode some time after 9 p.m. on the Tuesday. The following day, Kerruish heard that Kermode had not arrived at his final destination so he set off for Castletown and confirmed that the mail had been delivered at Kirk Santon and Ballasalla. Arriving in Castletown itself, he received news that Kermode had still not appeared so he went to help in the search for the missing man. Kerruish had looked in the fields and roads around King William's College, but had found nothing. It was later that day that he heard that Kermode's body had been found in the river.

Turning to the mail delivery system itself, Kerruish confirmed that until fairly recently the job of delivering the post to the various offices had belonged to a Mrs Shipley, but William Quiggin had tendered for it and been awarded the contract. Mr Quiggin had kept on the same drivers; however, there was a new driver on the Douglas to Castletown route. Hugh Flynn had been the former driver, but Kerruish understood that he had been dismissed and a new driver, John Kneen, appointed. On the Tuesday night, though, because the boat had been late, it had been Kermode who was detailed to take the bags. Finally, Kerruish was able to state that he was not aware of any ill-feeling between the dismissed Hugh Flynn and John Kermode.

Dr Cornelius Percy Ring said that he had first seen Kermode's body that very morning. He had made an examination and found a wound approximately three-quarters of an inch long on the right side of the back of the head, and examination of the inside of the skull showed a quantity of blood on the right side of the brain. The injury itself might have been caused by a fall, a blow or a kick from a horse.

The doctor was asked if it were possible that Kermode could have walked far after receiving such an injury. His body had been found some distance from the road he had been travelling on, and the inference was that he had been injured, walked off over the fields, and then collapsed into the river and possibly drowned. Dr Ring said that this could have happened if the bleeding had been slow enough, but added that he could not be sure if death was due to the blow Kermode had received, or from drowning.

Dr Ring went on to say that he had examined Kermode's cap and had found two tears on the inside, corresponding to the position of the head wound. These tears might have been caused by a blow from a stick or object with a sharp edge, or possibly even from a stone being thrown at Kermode. If these tears, and indeed the wound, had been caused by a fall, then their position meant that at some stage Kermode would have had to fall backwards.

Dr Samuel Laird had been present when Dr Ring carried out the postmortem; he agreed with the previous witness, but said that he felt that death had been due to drowning.

The coroner observed that at this stage the exact cause of death had not been determined; Dr Ring could not be sure if it had been due to the blow to the head or to drowning, and Dr Laird had felt that it had been as a result of drowning. As a result, Coroner Christian ordered that a second postmortem would be needed and asked that it be carried out at 10 a.m. the next day, by Dr Ring.

Daniel Flynn was the next witness. He stated that his son Hugh had tendered for the mail contract, but had not been successful. On the Tuesday in question he had been out with Hugh and they had arrived home, together, at around 6 p.m. Daniel had then gone out for a short time, and met up with William Quayle in the marketplace in Castletown.

At 8 p.m., Daniel and William had gone to a pub run by Thomas Chartres, where they had two half-glasses of rum before Daniel returned home, arriving there at 10 p.m. His son was in the house at that time and neither of them went out again that night. He confirmed that there was no ill-feeling whatsoever between his family and Kermode or anyone else involved in the mail contract. Finally, Daniel stated that his son had left the island on Friday, 19 January, to go to England, but he returned on the Saturday.

Hugh Flynn, Daniel's son, then took the stand, and confirmed that he had delivered the mail along the Douglas to Castletown route until William Quiggin had taken over the contract. Quiggin had discovered that Flynn had been carrying passengers and had dismissed him but, once again, claimed that there was no ill-feeling between them.

On the Tuesday, Hugh had left home, with his father, at about 10 a.m. They were out in the fields and returned home that evening. His father was home until 6 p.m., and he himself went out between 7 p.m. and 7.30 p.m. to visit Mrs Edwards who lived opposite to them in Castletown. Hugh returned home at about 8.30 p.m. and his father came in around 10 p.m. Neither of them had gone out again until the next day. Hugh stated that he had driven the mail cart for two years or so and been paid ten shillings a week. He ended his evidence by saying that he had gone to Liverpool on the Friday.

Edward Moore was the driver of the Castletown coach and he testified that he had known John Kermode and last seen him alive on Monday, 15 January. He had seen Kermode's body at around 3.10 p.m. on the Wednesday, very soon after it had been discovered. It lay in a place called the Claddagh, face down in the river. The water there was quite shallow and indeed just about covered the body. Kermode was fully clothed

Kirk Braddan where John Kermode was laid to restr

and still had his cap on with his arms folded underneath his chest. Moore was also able to say that he had seen the mail coach Kermode had been driving and noticed that the footboard was broken as if it had been stamped upon. The inquest was then adjourned until the following Tuesday. The following afternoon, John Kermode was laid to rest at Kirk Braddan. On Tuesday, 23 January, the inquest re-opened.

Interesting testimony was given by Stephen Fargher. At around 10.30 p.m. on the Tuesday he had been driving home from Castletown to Ballasalla and at one stage he passed the mail coach, though he took no real notice of it at the time. A minute or two later he heard some voices from the other side of the road, and saw a man, sitting on the grass, facing away from the road.

It was quite a stormy night so Fargher was not able to supply a description of the man, but he did shout to him and ask him what he was doing. The man mumbled something Fargher did not hear and then shouted, 'It's none of your business.' It was Fargher's impression that the man was talking to someone in the field.

At that point, Fargher heard someone approaching and saw that it was William Quarrie of Ballshick. He told Mr Quarrie what he had seen and said that he felt there was something wrong, adding that he believed the man might be in the process of stealing sheep. The two men went to look where the man had been sitting, but now there was no one to be seen.

James Mylchreest had been travelling from Douglas to his home in Castletown that same Tuesday night, and on the way he passed two men who looked as if they might be farm labourers. They were on the west side of Ballasalla Hill and one of the men appeared to be rather tipsy. Mylchreest was able to say that both men were wearing caps, and that one of them was quite tall and the other was of average build.

Dr Ring was recalled and, after performing the second post-mortem, was now convinced that death had been due to the head injury. He and Dr Laird had, however, found half a pint of water in Kermode's stomach, showing that he was still alive when he went into the water. There was, though, no water in the lungs which showed that death was not due to drowning. This was all confirmed by Dr Laird.

At this point, Dr Jones, who had testified at the first inquest, was recalled. He now claimed that he had seen the head injury when he made his examination, but could detect no fracture and did not believe that it had contributed to Kermode's death. Perhaps the general feeling about Dr Jones's prowess was best summed up by the coroner himself – who inquired if Jones had been sober when he had examined the body. Dr Jones said that he had been, but this was somewhat negated by the next witness, Matthias Caine, who had come to claim Kermode's body after that first inquest. In addition to saying what had happened at that time, Caine also said that Dr Jones did not look completely sober.

Mrs Edwards from Castletown was called to confirm that Hugh Flynn had been at her house at the time he had stated. Thomas Chartres, the publican, was then called and he said that although Daniel Flynn and William Quayle had been in his establishment on the Monday night, they had not been there on the Tuesday as Flynn had stated. This was then confirmed by William Quayle himself.

Sarah Flynn, Hugh's sister, said that she had gone across to Mrs Edwards's house at 11 p.m. to collect her brother. They went home together, and very soon afterwards Hugh went up to bed. Sarah saw him in bed later as they shared the same room. Her father was also in bed at the time, as Sarah had taken him in a drink as she retired.

Thomas Tyson, the postmaster at Ballasalla, said that Kermode had delivered the mail to him at 9.40 p.m. on the Tuesday and that there could not have been anything wrong with the foot-board of the coach at that time for Kermode stood on it while he passed the mail bag down to him.

Thomas Corrin told of his discovery of the mail cart on Tuesday night and of Kermode's body on Wednesday afternoon. He also said that when he had first gone to look for the missing driver, he had also found a rug on the eastern side of the road, a short distance away.

The final witness was Sergeant Hollinwraike, who said he had gone to the spot where the man had been seen by Stephen Fargher. He had walked across the fields from that spot to where the body had eventually been found and saw no trace of any footprints along the route.

On Tuesday, 30 January, the inquest opened again. The coroner began by stating that he had received a letter from Daniel Flynn saying that his evidence had been misrepresented in the newspapers. He went on to say that he had only 'thought' that he and William Quayle had been in the public house, but according to the newspapers he had stated this as a fact. He had witnesses who he wanted the coroner to call who would show where he had been, and claimed it was 'Douglas bigots' who had tried to cast a slur on himself and his son.

Dr Ring was then recalled. Two spots of what looked like blood had been found on the mail cart, behind the seat where the driver would have been. Dr Ring had tested this and confirmed that it was human blood. He had then sent the items to Dr Thomson of Kirk Michael, and he had agreed with Dr Ring's findings.

Edward Kissack of Howe Farm had known Kermode for twelve years and had even employed him in the past as a casual labourer. He described Kermode as a quiet, obliging man who was never bad tempered and always cheerful. Kissack thought it highly unlikely that Kermode would take his own life, and said he had never seen him under the influence of drink.

Henry Wesley Bell was a car proprietor and had been the direct employer of the dead man. On Tuesday, the 16th, Mr Quiggin had contacted Bell to ask if it would be all right for Kermode to make the delivery that evening. Henry Bell's final piece of evidence was that, from behind, Kermode looked very much like Mr Quiggin.

William Quiggin, of Church Street, Douglas, confirmed that he had obtained the contract to carry the mail after Mrs Shipley had given it up. That was on 3 September 1865. There had been other tenders at the time, from Henry Wesley Bell and Hugh Flynn. He was later informed that he and Flynn had tendered exactly the same amount, but that he had been successful.

Quiggin said that he had dismissed Hugh Flynn some four or five weeks before Kermode's death, for carrying passengers on the mail coach. On Tuesday, 16 January, he had originally asked John Flynn, a cousin of Hugh, if he could drive the cart that night. John had said he would for one shilling, but ten minutes later had changed his mind and said he would only do it for an extra sixpence. Quiggin had refused and said he would get one of Wesley Bell's drivers to do it instead.

From there, Quiggin had gone to Kermode's home and asked him if he would do it. Kermode asked him what time he thought he might get home and Quiggin had replied that it would be some time between midnight and 1 a.m. Finally, Quiggin told the court that the mail bags in the cart would be kept under the driver's seat and could only be removed by someone standing on the foot-board.

Henry Gale then took the stand and gave a rambling account

of hearing Hugh Flynn making threats against Quiggin. This had been some five weeks before Kermode's death and was about the time Hugh had been dismissed. Flynn had also said he would do violence to anyone who took the mail cart to Castletown. This testimony was given even less credence when Gale was unable to pick out Hugh Flynn in court. At the end of his evidence, Daniel Flynn stood and asked for Gale to be charged with wilful and corrupt perjury, but the coroner refused. The inquest was then adjourned again, to the following day.

On Wednesday, the last day of January, John Waterson, a schoolmaster, stated that he had gone to Chartres' public house at around 9.45 p.m. on Tuesday, the 16th, and had seen Daniel Flynn there.

John Kennaugh, a farmer, had also been in the same public house. He had arrived at 9.30 p.m. and some time later, at about 10.55 p.m., he had seen Daniel Flynn there.

Edward Corlett was another publican at Castletown and he told the court that Daniel Flynn had been in his establishment between about 10 p.m. and 10.50 p.m. on that night.

These three witnesses had, in effect, said that Flynn was in two public houses at the same time but, taken together, they seemed to indicate that he had been out drinking in Castletown at the time John Kermode had been attacked.

The coroner summed up, castigating Daniel Flynn for what was, in effect, contempt of court the previous day. He then summed up the facts of the case saying that there were basically three verdicts open to the jury: accident, suicide or murder. A verdict of accident was inconsistent with the wound on the head and other factors, and suicide was improbable. He ended by criticizing Dr Jones and pointing out that his evidence was most unsatisfactory.

The jury retired at 4.05 p.m. and, after thirty minutes, returned to give the only possible verdict: 'Wilful murder against some person or persons unknown.' No one was ever brought to justice for the murder.

4
The Last Execution

In the year 1872 there were just three houses in Glen Moar, Sulby Glen. The topmost of these houses was occupied by Thomas Kewish and his family, and in the middle one lived Thomas's father, John Kewish, his wife Mary, and their other two children – John Kewish junior and a sister who was never named at the time. In the third house lived John Craine, his wife Margaret, and their family.

Things were not as they should have been in that middle house in Glen Moar. In fact, the Kewish family had split into two factions. This had all come about because of two disagreements: one between John Kewish and his son, John junior, and one between John and his wife, Mary.

In the very early part of the year, John junior owed his father money and either wasn't in a position to repay it or simply chose not too. Eventually the matter was sorted out and John promised to give his father a cow and a small parcel of land that he owned, both to be handed over in May. At about the same time, Mary had argued with her husband and now she, her son and her daughter lived in one part of the house while John Kewish senior lived in another.

Things continued in this vein until Monday, 28 March 1872. In the early evening of that date, Margaret Craine, John Kewish junior and a man named Hugh Kneen were walking up Glen Moar towards Thomas's house. As they reached the middle house, John went inside, leaving the other two to go on to Thomas's. As Margaret and Hugh passed the middle house they heard Mary inside, talking to her husband. This confirmed that at this particular time, Mary, her husband and her son were the only people inside the house as the sister was already at Thomas's and would spend the night there.

Some ten minutes after this, Mary Kewish also arrived at Thomas's house, leaving just John Kewish senior and his son in the middle house. That would be the case for about one hour because it was then that John Kewish junior also arrived at Thomas's house.

There followed some discussion over why John hadn't come earlier. Thomas was in the process of killing a pig; John Kewish junior had known this, and had offered to help. Thomas asked his brother why he was so late but John did not reply and, if anything, seemed to be much quieter than usual.

As the evening unfolded, Mary Kewish asked her son John if she should go home and prepare supper for them. John said that she should, and in due course Mary, Margaret Craine and Hugh Kneen left together to walk back down the lane. Mary then went inside her own house as the other two walked on.

The first thing Mary did was to light a fire in her room and start preparing supper, and she would later estimate that she spent around an hour carrying out this task. It was only then that she noticed that the door to her husband's room was open. Usually he kept it closed, so Mary went inside to see if he was about.

John Kewish senior was indeed in his room. He was in a kneeling position in front of one of his chairs and leaning over it. He was clearly dead and Mary could see a number of wounds on his body. Without further delay, she dashed to John Craine's house for assistance.

Margaret Craine and Mary returned to Mary's house together with a man named William Kneale. Details of what had been discovered were passed on to Thomas Kewish, and he too – along with his brother John – went to his father's house after finding John Craine himself, who accompanied him. It was John Craine and William Kneale who made a careful examination of the scene.

There were four puncture wounds on John Kewish's back and two more on his chest. It looked as if some instrument like a pitchfork had inflicted these wounds and indeed there was such an implement standing against a wooden partition in the room. During this time, John Kewish junior remained out of the way, in the kitchen, and shortly afterwards Mary Kewish walked through the room where the body lay and into the kitchen herself. It was at that stage that Kneale heard Mary say, in Manx: 'I hope Johnny has not done anything to him' – though he was unable to say who in particular she might have been speaking to at the time.

The first surprise in this case came when it was suggested that the authorities would have to be involved and an investigation and an inquest held. Neither Mary nor her son John seemed too interested in this idea and made it plain that they intended simply to bury the body and get on with their lives. This information found its way to the authorities, and at noon on Sunday, 3 April, some visitors arrived at the Kewish home.

Those visitors were: the High Bailiff of Ramsey, William Boyd; the chief constable, Constable Thomas Kneale; Dr F. S. Tellett of Ramsey; and the coroner. They arrived to find John Kewish's body laid out ready for burial and discovered that the funeral was to be held that very afternoon. This was immediately halted and an inquest into the circumstances surrounding John's death opened. After the basic details had been given, the proceedings were adjourned until the following day. That same Sunday afternoon, a postmortem examination was carried out by Dr Tellett and Dr Clucas.

It was also on the Sunday, after the house had been searched, that the authorities found John Kewish's sister in one of the rooms. She was covered in rags and obviously suffering from severe mental problems. She was consequently taken into care and confined to an asylum.

The inquest reopened on Monday, 4 April, and the first witnesses were the two doctors. Dr Tellett reported the six separate wounds – two on the right side of the chest and four more on the back. These wounds had caused the right lung to collapse and, as a result, the chest cavity had filled with blood. One had penetrated the aorta and would have caused instantaneous death. The wounds had square edges, and both doctors believed that these wounds had been caused by a two-pronged instrument, used with a good deal of force.

Dr Clucas agreed with Dr Tellett's testimony, but added the interesting fact that the shirt, found on the floor near the body, bore holes in the back but none in the front. Five of the wounds had penetrated the lungs with the final one penetrating the aorta. Any of the six would have proved fatal.

Another important witness was Constable Thomas Kneale who had been appointed to guard the outside of the cottage. He said that he had heard Mary Kewish and her son John talking in Manx. John had told his mother, 'Take care to be steady on your oath for if we get today over it will shut people's mouths and there will be no more of it.' Later still, Constable Kneale had been speaking to John who had said that his father deserved what he had got.

This behaviour and the fact that John had been left alone with his father for a full hour was held to be highly suspicious. The verdict, when it came, was that the jury felt that John should stand trial for the murder of his father. Immediately, John Kewish was cautioned and told of the charge of murder. In reply he said, 'I never laid a hand on him. I was not there when it was done.'

A few days after this, on 9 April, a further search of the Kewish house was made. During this search, a gun was found, concealed in the thatch of a roof. The gun was free from rust and appeared only to have been hidden very recently.

Although John was now held at Castle Rushen to await his trial for murder, there was another matter to be dealt with first. John was a well-known sheep stealer in the area and on Tuesday, 16 April, he was brought before the court at Ramsey to face that charge. He was found guilty, but no sentence was imposed at that time as the more serious charge had yet to be heard.

Castle Rushen where John Kewish faced his trial

The trial of John Kewish opened at Castle Rushen on Tuesday, 11 June 1872. The case for the prosecution was put by the Attorney General, while Kewish was defended by Mr Steven and Mr Quayle.

In the early stages of the trial the possibility of another killer was put forward. There had been rumours that Mary Kewish might have been responsible for her husband's death. After all, she too had been left alone with him in the house, for about an hour, while she had been preparing the supper. The court was told that this might well form a part of John Kewish's defence, but the jury should remember two things. First, the blood was almost dry when the body was viewed by the neighbours, implying that the attack had taken place some time before. Second, considerable force must have been used to inflict the wounds and it was held that Mary was simply not capable.

Testimony was given that the prisoner had, at one stage, owned a small pitchfork with prongs some 3 inches apart. This weapon had never been found and indeed this was what officers were looking for on 9 April when the gun had been found hidden in the thatch.

Mary Kewish told the court that before she left for Thomas's house, which was some 400 yards from her own, she had given her husband some milk. She was in the street as Margaret Craine and Hugh Kneen passed her house on their way to Thomas's and followed them a few minutes later. It would have been between 7 p.m. and 8 p.m. and she stayed at Thomas's for about an hour. After returning to her own house she had taken a can down to the river to get some water. By the time she found her husband's body it would have been after 10 p.m.

Thomas Kewish told the court that at some time between 7 p.m. and 8 p.m. on the day his father was murdered, he had killed a pig. Soon after this, his mother came to visit, and about an hour after that, his brother John arrived. Later, after the body had been found and Thomas had gone to his father's house, he asked John if had done something to him. John replied that he hadn't seen his father all day.

Thomas gave one other most interesting piece of information. Other witnesses would report that a pitchfork was seen, lying against a partition, in the room where the murder took place. Thomas was able to say that this did not belong to the family.

William Kneale testified that at 11 p.m. or thereabouts, Thomas Kewish had come to his house and told him his father was dead. William immediately went to the Kewish house and found that John's body was not yet cold. He was in the kitchen, over an armchair near the fireplace, with his hands on the seat. He was lying face down and his upper torso was naked. Blood was still flowing from the wounds and near the body lay a blood-covered shirt.

John Craine said that it was some time between 10 p.m. and 11 p.m. when Thomas Kewish had come to his house, told him that John was dead, and asked him to come back to the house with him. By the time he got there, William Kneale was already in attendance, and by now John Kewish's body was lying on the floor. Craine had stayed in the Kewish house all that night but neither Mary Kewish nor her son John seemed to care about what had happened.

Robert Corlett was a mason and he had spoken to Mary Kewish on the morning of Monday, 28 March. Robert asked about her husband and Mary said that he had gone to Ramsey but she didn't know why. She went on to say that she wished her son would give him a thrashing but added, 'It's no use touching him unless he gave him something to settle him at once.'

Margaret Craine said that as she, Hugh Kneen and John Kewish passed the middle house in the lane, John Kewish senior was standing in the doorway to the kitchen. There was no one else on the street. This was in direct contradiction to the testimony given by Mary Kewish. After hearing about the body being found, Margaret had gone to Thomas Kewish's house to tell him what had taken place. As she arrived, John was just coming out so she told him about his father's death. He did not seem surprised.

Hugh Kneen agreed with Margaret Craine that when they passed the Kewish house on their way to Thomas's, Mary was not in the street outside.

William Kermode was a jailer at the Castle Rushen prison and he told the court that John had told him a story about how his father had died. According to John, his father had taken off his coat and waistcoat to fight with a man who had then stabbed him in the chest with a pitchfork. His father had fallen forward and the other man had then stabbed him twice more in the back. Little credence was given to this story.

Constable Daniel Cowley had made a search of the Kewish house and found a pair of russet-coloured trousers which the accused had worn on the day that his father died. There were bloodstains on the trousers, but Cowley carelessly left them in one particular room while he carried on with his search. When he returned to that room, the trousers had gone. They were only found some days later when they were handed back to him by Mary Kewish. The stains were much less pronounced now and it was obvious that the garment had been washed in the meantime.

The jury retired to consider their verdict but returned after one hour to say that they were hopelessly deadlocked. The case was then adjourned until the following day but, after further deliberation, they were still unable to reach a verdict. Seven had wished to say that Kewish was not guilty, while the remaining five had voted him guilty. The jury was discharged and a new trial ordered.

That second trial took place on Wednesday, 3 July, and this time the jury had no problem in deciding that Kewish was guilty as charged. He was then sentenced to death and returned to his cell to await his fate.

John Kewish continued to deny that he was responsible for his father's death. His brother Thomas visited him in prison and urged him to confess his guilt mainly because their mother was still subject to much suspicion. Finally, on Sunday, 14 July, John Kewish said that he wished to discuss something. He then made a full statement confessing to the murder of his father.

We will return to a discussion of this statement later. For now, suffice to say that John admitted that he had gone into the kitchen of the house where his father was and asked him to pass him down a gun which was kept on a mount above the fireplace. His father did so and the trigger must have caught on something for it went off. There had been four slugs in the gun and this had caused the six wounds seen on his body. Two of the slugs had passed directly through his father, thus causing four wounds on his back and two on his chest. John had then taken the gun and hidden it in the thatch of an outhouse before going on to his brother Thomas's house. Later still, John made a second statement in which he admitted that he had fired the gun deliberately into his father's body.

Attempts were made now to show that John was insane and had not known what he was doing. Medical opinion, though, was that he did indeed know right from wrong and his confession showed that the act was deliberate.

John Kewish's fate was now sealed. The authorities asked their counterparts in England for a suitable man to perform the execution and William Calcraft was subsequently asked to carry out the task.

It had been forty years since there had been an execution on the island and it was soon found that the existing scaffold was not suitable for the job. A new one had to be built, but the carpenters of the area refused to carry out this task. Furthermore, since it had been so long since the last time a gallows had been used, there were no plans available for the new construction. In the end, new plans were obtained and it was with some difficulty that the apparatus was built by some local boys.

There remain some unanswered questions in the case of John Kewish. Evidence had been given that there were holes in the dead man's bloodstained shirt, which had been found near his body. The wounds, however they might have been inflicted, would have caused instant death. Who then removed John's shirt, and why?

Second, two eminent doctors had examined the body and performed a detailed postmortem. They reported square-shaped wounds. These were hardly consistent with a shooting but could well have been inflicted by a pitchfork, as originally thought.

Third, those same doctors did not report the finding of any slugs or other shot in John Kewish's body. If four slugs were fired into him they might possibly have caused six wounds, two of them being exit wounds, but that meant that two would have still been inside John Kewish. Further, there was no report of any slugs being found in the murder room, though it is possible that these could have been removed in the week or so between the murder and the involvement of the authorities.

There was also the matter of Kewish's sister. Thomas and other witnesses said that she had been at his house, 'helping out', yet this same woman was later certified and placed in an asylum. What possible assistance could such a person have been offering in Thomas's house?

Finally, Mary Kewish had obviously lied. For some reason she claimed to have been outside in the street as her neighbours passed her house on the way to Thomas's. Those neighbours all agreed that she was not there. Why had she lied about what seems such an innocuous matter?

There can be little doubt that John Kewish was killed by at least two thrusts, possibly three, from a two-pronged pitchfork. After death, his shirt was removed and thrown to the floor. It may well have been John Kewish junior who committed that crime, but why did he then confess to a shooting that never actually took place?

Whatever the truth, the executioner, Calcraft, duly arrived on the island and, on Thursday, 1 August 1872, John Kewish was hanged on the new scaffold in the Debtor's Yard at Castle Rushen, his body being buried afterwards in the Stone Yard.

John Kewish earned his place in history by being the last man ever to suffer death by hanging on the Isle of Man.

5

A Nice Weekend Break

On 14 March 1882, George Barker James Cooper argued with his wife Edith at their home in Altrincham. So heated did the altercation become that at one stage George drew out a pistol, aimed and fired. Fortunately for Edith, the wound she sustained did not prove fatal, but George still found himself arrested and charged with attempted murder. On 24 April, he appeared before Mr Justice Chitty and was, perhaps surprisingly, acquitted. Soon afterwards, George and his wife divorced.

A few years after this, towards the end of 1888, another woman with the same name – Edith Cooper – left her home in Birmingham and took employment at the Central Hotel in Douglas. By coincidence, George Cooper often travelled to the Isle of Man as his family had property there, and so it was that the two met and started walking out together. One thing led to another and, in November 1891, the couple married in Shirley. The newlyweds, now living at 3 West Clyne, Stretford, Manchester, often returned to the island, sometimes on business, sometimes for a pleasant break, and always stayed at the Regent Hotel on the Loch Promenade.

On Friday, 2 September 1892, George and Edith Cooper travelled to Douglas on the *Mona's Queen* from Fleetwood and arrived at the Regent Hotel just before 7 p.m. The crossing, apparently, had been rather rough and Edith was still feeling quite ill. In fact, Edith was so bad that she had to lie down for a short time in room 11 before the chambermaid, Mary O'Brien, showed her and George to room 16 where they

The Mona's Queen, *the steamship on which George and Edith Cooper travelled to the island on 2 September 1892*

would be staying. At one stage, Mary even had to bring Edith a glass of brandy and water to revive her.

Once she was in room 16, Edith lay down on the bed and Mary asked her if she might bring her a cup of tea. Edith politely declined saying that she didn't require anything else. At that, Mary O'Brien left the couple to unpack and continued her own duties.

At around 9 p.m., George Cooper was seen outside the front door of the hotel. One hour later, at 10 p.m. he was observed returning to the hotel and going up to his room. For a while at least, nothing more was heard from room 16.

At 3.30 a.m. on the Saturday morning, George was downstairs, asking for some champagne. Told that the bar was closed at that rather ungodly hour, he settled for a soda water which he then took up to his bedroom.

Some four and a half hours later, George Cooper was in the dining room enjoying breakfast. Edith, perhaps still suffering from the after-effects of the sea crossing, remained in bed. Thirty minutes later, at 9 a.m., George left the Regent but returned soon afterwards with John Champion Bradshaw, a local photographer and artist. George was heard asking Bradshaw if he would take a glass of champagne. The two gentlemen then entered the Smoke Room whereupon George excused himself and said he had to go up to his room. John Bradshaw waited in the Smoke Room for twenty minutes or so and, when George still hadn't returned, left the hotel.

At this same time, Mary O'Brien was busily cleaning the various bedrooms and, at 10.30 a.m., was in room 19 when she thought she heard a slight scream. Soon afterwards Mary was in room 18 when she heard what sounded like someone falling out of bed in room 16, the one occupied by the Coopers. Curious, Mary walked to the door of room 16, crouched down, and peered through the keyhole. What she saw alarmed her: Edith Cooper was lying naked on the floor between the bed and the washstand and her husband George was leaning over her, a towel in his hand, wiping Edith's face.

This required further investigation so Mary sent one of the other chambermaids, Jane Cronin, to fetch someone. In due

The Regent Hotel where George Cooper murdered his wife in 1892

course, Mrs Sarah Anne Jones, the manageress, and Miss Mary Keeling, the book-keeper, knocked on the door and asked if anything was wrong, adding that the noise from within was disturbing the house. At one stage, Mrs Jones asked if the Coopers might require anything and, from within, George answered the single word 'no'. The room had, however, gone quiet now so the two ladies returned to their duties and Mary O'Brien continued with her cleaning.

At some time between 11 a.m. and 11.30 a.m., Mary was in room 2, which was directly below room 16. Once again there was noise from the room above and again it sounded as if someone had fallen on to the floor. Mary now took her concerns to Mr Welden, the manager, who went up to the room with the head porter, Gilbert Connock.

William Welden knocked briskly on the door and demanded to be admitted. There was no reply. Welden knocked for a second time and now, slowly, George Cooper opened the door. Edith lay on the floor, her feet underneath the bed, and she appeared to be unconscious. Connock went to her and turned her slightly, and only now did he see a wound close to her breast. Taking charge, Welden sent Connock to fetch a doctor and the police.

Constable John Henry Whitfield was on the promenade at 11.45 a.m. when Connock approached him and said that a woman had been injured in the hotel. Whitfield immediately dashed to room 16 at the Regent, examined Edith, and discovered that she was dead. He asked, 'Who has done this?' and George Cooper replied, 'I don't know. I have been to Dumbell's Bank in company with Mr Bradshaw and on my return I found her like this.'

Whitfield continued, 'Did you find her like this?'

Cooper replied, 'No, she was in bed in a faint.' Shortly after, following Dr Joseph O'Malley's arrival, Cooper announced, 'I want to go downstairs for a drink. I can't stand this.' He was immediately informed by Constable Whitfield that he was not allowed to leave the room. Soon afterwards

*The Central Hotel in Douglas where George Cooper met
his second wife, Edith*

George Cooper was arrested and charged with the wilful murder of his wife.

The inquest opened that same afternoon, at the Regent Hotel, before Mr Samuel Harris, the coroner for Douglas. The first witness was William Welden, who testified that George Cooper and his wife had visited the hotel three times within the last year. He confirmed that he had started his own duties at 7.30 a.m. that morning and had first seen Mr Cooper at around 8.30 a.m. when they had spoken briefly near to the hotel's front door. At the time, he said, Cooper appeared calm and sober though he was aware that a small bottle of champagne had been sent up to room 16 earlier that morning.

Welden went on to say that he had first heard of the noises and commotion from room 16 at about 10 a.m. but that it was on the second occasion, more than an hour later, when he and the porter went up to investigate. Upon entering the room he saw Edith lying naked on the floor, on her left side, close to the bed. At the time, George Cooper was on the bed, fully clothed, though his collar was somewhat disarranged. Cooper had made no remark when informed later that his wife was dead.

The next witness was John Bradshaw. He stated that he had been commissioned by Cooper to prepare two portraits of Edith. On the Friday, he had had an appointment with Cooper, but when Bradshaw called at the hotel Cooper was not there. He called twice and then left a message asking Cooper to call on him the next day.

On the Saturday, Cooper had arrived at around 9.30 a.m. but Bradshaw was busy so the two did not actually meet until around 9.50 a.m. They drove together to Dumbell's Bank on Prospect Hill where Cooper paid the account owed for the two pictures and then they drove on to the hotel. Bradshaw went on to detail the offer of champagne, the adjournment to the Smoke Room, Cooper going up to his bedroom and then, once he had grown tired of waiting, his own departure after leaving a message that he could not wait any longer. Finally, Bradshaw stated that, at this time, he did not believe Cooper to be sober. The inquest was then adjourned until the next day, Monday, at 10.30 a.m.

In the event, no evidence was actually heard on the Monday, because at the start of the hearing the coroner announced that two telegrams had been received – one from Edith's father and one from George's father. Both men had expressed a desire to attend and hear the evidence for themselves. As a result, the proceedings were adjourned again, until the following day.

The first witness on Tuesday, 6 September, was Mary O'Brien – who was better known as Polly. She stated that she had worked at the hotel for three years. After detailing the arrival of the Coopers on the Friday and Edith's apparent illness from the crossing, Polly turned to Saturday, the day of Edith's death.

At about 8 a.m., Polly had been on the second floor landing when George Cooper came out of his room and asked her to get him a collar stud. She said she had one and gave it to him.

Later that same morning, Cooper ordered a small bottle of champagne and it had been Polly who took it up to his room. Cooper took the bottle from her and poured out two glasses. He drank one down quickly and offered her the second one. She refused.

As she was about to leave, Cooper mentioned again that his wife was very ill. She had then gone into room 16 and saw Edith, wearing her nightdress, lying on the bed. Polly enquired after her health and Edith replied that she was still sick. It was soon after this, while she was cleaning room 14, that another chambermaid came to her and said that she had heard raised voices and thought that the Coopers were arguing. When Polly heard the sound of someone falling out of bed whilst cleaning room 18 she went to look through the keyhole; by now, Mrs Cooper was lying naked on the floor near the bed and her husband appeared to be ministering to her.

Dr O'Malley was the next to give his evidence. He said that after he had pronounced 'life extinct', Edith's body had been lifted on to the bed and he noticed that there were bruises on her right forearm. There was no blood on the floor of the bedroom, but the carpet was wet. The police had shown Dr O'Malley a penknife, one blade of which was open; he had noticed that it was stained with blood and was clearly very sharp indeed.

Later that Saturday, Dr O'Malley had performed the post-mortem with Dr Buxton and Dr Woods. He noted bruises on both legs, which appeared to be long-standing ones. More recent bruising was noticed on the arms and both eyes. These bruises might well have been caused by blows, he said. As for the fatal stab wound, it had passed through the left lung and the pulmonary artery had been pierced. There was no possibility that the wound had been self-inflicted.

Dr Thomas Woods was the next witness to be called and he agreed entirely with the findings of Dr O'Malley. It was then the turn of Miss Tillie Yeaman to give her evidence.

Miss Yeaman worked at the hotel and had seen the Coopers arrive on the Friday. At the time, Edith was perfectly sober, though she did seem to be suffering from the effects of a rough sea voyage. Later that evening, she had seen George Cooper and asked after his wife's health. Cooper had replied that he had given her a good thrashing with a horsewhip the night before. Miss Yeaman was most upset by this and asked why, if he felt this way, he didn't simply leave his wife. Cooper replied, 'Oh no! I will pay the devil out in a better way than that.' Later still, she saw him taking a glass of sherry at the bar and he did not appear to be sober. It had been Miss Yeaman to whom Mr Bradshaw had given his message on the Saturday morning that he couldn't wait any longer for Cooper and he had left the hotel at around 10.45 a.m.

Mary Keeling then detailed her visit to room 16 on the Saturday morning and of asking the Coopers to be quiet as they were disturbing the other guests. She recalled that there was no answer from within, but the noise did cease.

Mary was followed to the stand by Gilbert Connock, the head porter. He had originally gone to the boat to meet the Coopers on the Friday, but had missed them and saw them both at the hotel soon afterwards. He then went on to describe his visit to room 16 in the company of Mr Welden and of his subsequent finding of Constable Whitfield on the promenade. Later he had sent one of the porters for the doctor, while he himself ran to the police station to tell Inspector Cain what had happened. After Connock's evidence was heard, the inquest was adjourned again, this time to Thursday, 8 September.

On the Thursday, the first witness called was John Alexander Clarke, a steward on the *Mona's Queen*, the ship the Coopers had travelled on to the island. He stated that the couple had a private cabin. The sea on that trip had been very heavy and a number of passengers had suffered as a result. During the trip, Clarke took dinner to the Coopers. George took his meal; Edith didn't, but both of them had a glass of brandy.

Clarke was followed by Constable Whitfield. He reported the various conversations with Cooper in room 16. He also told the court what he found inside that room. On the floor, close to the foot of the bed, he found a lady's nightdress. There was blood on the breast and the garment had been cut down the middle and then ripped down to the bottom. One sleeve had been entirely torn off. On the washstand was a basin, three parts filled with blood and water. The penknife used in the attack had been found on a marble slab near the washstand. Finally, a gentleman's shirt had been found in the wardrobe. It had been saturated with water, but both wristbands were still bloody.

Sarah Anne Jones, the hotel manageress, then told the court of her visit to room 16 in the company of Mary Keeling, and was followed to the stand by Margaret Widdowson, who worked at the Athol Hotel. She confirmed that George Cooper had called at the hotel at around 9 a.m. on the Saturday and taken a glass of rum and milk.

The final witness was Inspector John Cain, who outlined a search he had made of the scene with Constable Thomas Warren. They had found some human hair on the bed and Cain testified that it looked as if it had been pulled out rather than cut.

A verdict of wilful murder against George Cooper was returned and the accused was then committed for trial. A hearing followed before Deemster Drinkwater on 27 September to determine whether Cooper should be sent for trial on a charge of murder, manslaughter, or even if he should be discharged. The six-man jury confirmed that the charge should be one of wilful murder.

The trial of George Cooper opened on Monday, 14 November, before the lieutenant governor of the island, Mr Spencer Walpole, Deemsters Drinkwater and Gell, and the clerk of the rolls, Mr Dumbell. Mr James S. Gell and Mr J. M. Cruickshank appeared for the prosecution, while Cooper was defended by Mr Thomas Kneed and Mr G. A. Ring. The proceedings would last for six days.

In addition to those already mentioned, both sides called

witnesses who gave most interesting details of the back-grounds of both George and Edith Cooper.

For the prosecution, Louisa Mary Cooper, the dead woman's sister, testified that the previous New Year's Day she had gone to stay with them at their house, which at that time was in Higher Broughton. Edith was sporting two black eyes and a bruise on her forehead.

William Henry Cooper, Edith's brother, had also stayed with the accused. While he was there, George and Edith had argued, and so heated had this become that he was forced to step in, necessitating him hitting George several times. A few days later, William had seen George hit Edith in the eye. As a result, William had thrashed George with a riding whip. Evidence was also given that Cooper might well have been involved with another woman, a Mrs Hunt of New Brighton. Indeed, her husband, Arthur Earle Hunt, was in the process of divorcing his wife and he too had once given George Cooper a severe thrashing because of his involvement with his wife.

One of the final prosecution witnesses was Sergeant James Bell who had been present when Cooper was formally charged at the police station. Cooper had been heard to reply, 'It is a sure case of suicide.'

By now, a picture had been painted of a brutal wife-beater, involved with another woman, who had perhaps been drinking too much and killed a wife he had been abusing for some time. It was now time for the defence to give their version of events.

Another steward, Henry Buckingham, who worked on the *Peveril*, testified that some three weeks before her death, Edith and George had travelled to the island on his boat. Edith had been drinking very heavily and was quite intoxicated by the time the boat docked. He also stated that, as far as he knew, George had always behaved kindly towards his wife.

Allan Pearson worked at the Athol Hotel which was next door to the Regent on Loch Promenade and he had known Edith quite well as she had lived with his mother for some time after she had left her employment at the Central Hotel in 1888.

He testified that Edith was often drunk and also had a very nasty temper indeed.

George Cooper confirmed that he had left the hotel on the morning of his wife's death, and walked to the Athol where he had a glass of rum and milk. After breakfast he returned to his room and asked his wife if she wished to have a cup of tea. She had said that she would prefer a glass of champagne which he then ordered. He took a glass for himself and placed his wife's on the washstand before leaving to see Mr Bradshaw.

After their business was concluded, he and Bradshaw returned to the hotel and Cooper went up to his room. Edith was still in bed, and he asked her if she would now get up as they had agreed to go to Sulby that afternoon. Edith replied that she hadn't come to the island to pay visits, and an argument then started in which she said one or two unkind things to him. These words caused him to lose his temper making the argument even worse.

At one stage, he had gone to the washstand and saw the penknife lying there, with one blade opened. He picked up the knife, intending to use it to clean his fingernails, and sat down on the side of the bed next to her.

George asked Edith if she would take some breakfast and, when she declined, he mentioned that the rolling of the ship they had travelled on, and the wine she had drunk, might have disagreed with her. At this, Edith barked, 'Do you call me a drunkard?'

As further words were exchanged, George felt a sharp blow on the side of his head and his glasses were knocked off. He turned and hit Edith back, but he did not recall that he had the knife in his hand. Edith gave a slight scream and said that George had cut her. Only now did he see the blood on her night-dress, but assumed that it was nothing more than a scratch.

Edith seemed to be falling back into a faint, so George took a cloth from the washstand and bathed her face with it. This is perhaps the sight that Mary O'Brien had seen as she looked through the keyhole of the door.

Continuing his narrative, George said that he tried to lift his wife out of bed and take her to the washstand but, in lifting her, saw that her feet fell heavily to the floor. He then removed her nightdress so that he would find it easier to bathe her and it was as he was doing so that Mr Welden knocked on the door and demanded to be admitted.

On the sixth day, the jury retired and after one hour and forty-five minutes returned to announce that they had found Cooper guilty of manslaughter, whereupon he was sentenced to ten years in prison.

The verdict was not well accepted by the general public. As the jury members left the court they were booed by an unfriendly mob and had to be protected by the police. Even when two of the judges left, they too were met by hissing. It seemed that as far as the people were concerned, justice had certainly not been done.

6

The Later Nineteenth Century (1851–99)

This chapter covers the other cases of murder or manslaughter, and other death sentences, between the years 1850 and 1899. There follow some details on these other crimes.

James Kewley – 1859

James Kewley was a tailor by trade, but illness had prevented him from working for some time. Consequently, he had fallen into financial difficulties. Separated from his wife, Kewley had a two-year-old daughter, Melvina Annie, to take care of and he found it increasingly difficult to make ends meet.

Kewley lived with his parents in Onchan and in mid-1859 believed that he had come up with a solution as far as taking care of his daughter was concerned. He took the child to John and Jane Creer, who lived in Douglas, and asked them if they would take care of Melvina if he paid them two shillings and nine pence every week. The Creers agreed, but by August had asked that the payments be increased. Kewley agreed to a new sum of three shillings, but soon fell into arrears – so much so that, by the end of August, Jane Creer called at Kewley's home to ask for the money she was owed. It was Kewley's mother who paid over the outstanding balance. A new solution needed to be found, it seemed.

In September, Kewley called on the Creers and admitted that he was unable to pay for his daughter's upkeep.

Fortunately, he had found a family who lived on the north of the island who would take Melvina without expecting any payment whosoever. He informed Jane Creer that he would call in due course to pick up his daughter.

In fact, Kewkey collected his daughter on Tuesday, 27 September, returning a couple of days later, with a trunk, to collect her clothing and other belongings. When the Creers asked about Melvina, Kewley confirmed that she was happy and well and being taken care of by his relatives. Jane Creer could not help but notice, though, that he appeared to be agitated and in a hurry to get away. Before he left, however, he did inform the Creers that he intended going away to sea.

On the afternoon of Sunday, 9 October, 13-year-old Robert Killip was playing near the Mill Dam on Howstrake Farm in Onchan when he noticed something floating in the water. Taking a long stick, Robert tried to pull it towards the bank when the object rolled over to reveal that it was the fully clothed body of a young girl. Killip shouted for help to James Quayle who lived nearby, and it was he who finally retrieved the tragic bundle, which was taken to the Nursery Inn.

By Wednesday, 12 October, when the inquest opened before the deputy coroner, Mr Senhouse Wilson, the poor girl had been identified as Melvina Kewley and the search was on for her father who had gone missing from his parents' house.

Jane Creer told the court that she recognized the body as that of Melvina and confirmed that the clothing she wore was the same as she had on when her father collected her on 27 September. She was also able to say that before Melvina left her home, she had been given a meal of bread, milk and tea.

It was clear that Melvina had never been handed over to any other relatives and had almost certainly died on the same day she had been handed back to her father. John Kewley, James's father, said that he had not seen the child since August nor seen James himself since 30 September.

Dr Cornelius Percy Ring had examined the body and performed a postmortem. He reported a wound on the left side of Melvina's head, consistent with a blow from some object with a sharpened edge. Further examination showed that the skull was fractured and there were signs of a meal having been consumed some two to three hours before death. That meal consisted of bread, milk and some tea and this was consistent with what Jane Creer had given the child on 27 September. Finally, Dr Ring said that Melvina had been in the water for some ten to fourteen days.

It did not take the jury long to announce that Melvina had been murdered by her father, James Kewley, and it was then that the newspapers revealed that no search for him abroad or on boats would be carried out as there were not sufficient funds available to cover the cost. As a result, James Kewley was never found and did not stand trial for the murder of his daughter.

Patrick Gallagher – 1864

Patrick Gallagher had made a success of his life. By the early 1860s, he was not only the landlord of the Albert public house in Douglas, but he also ran a lucrative business as a coach driver between Douglas and Ramsey. Life was good until a rival company, Smyth's Coaches, also began running a service between the two towns. Not only that, but they were cheaper and faster; soon, Gallagher found that business dropped off to almost nothing.

Both coach companies operated their services from the quayside at Douglas and, on Saturday, 10 December 1864, were due to leave at about the same time. Gallagher drove his own coach, which had no passengers and just two small parcels to carry. His rival's coach was driven by one William Kennish, but also on board that coach was Edwin Wilmot who acted as a tout for Smyth's Coaches, encouraging people to travel on his employer's coach. There was little love lost between Gallagher and Wilmot.

On this particular morning, words were exchanged between

The north quayside in Douglas from where Patrick Gallagher's coach, and that of his rival, started

the two men before the coaches set off for Ramsey. William Berey had offices on the north quay and the coach stop was directly outside. At 9.55 a.m., he heard some sort of argument outside. He could not tell what was actually said, but did see Wilmot abusing Gallagher and taunting him. It was Gallagher's coach that set off first, and Berey saw Wilmot try to grab the reins of the horses in order to stop them. Moments later, the other coach, driven by Kennish with Wilmot sitting next to him, had also set off.

Even though Gallagher had left first, and Kennish had to stop to pick up another passenger, they were still catching up Gallagher's coach. Finally, in Finch Road, Gallagher fell behind and Wilmot laughed at him as they passed. The two coaches continued and, as they turned the corner out of Finch Road, Wilmot turned again and laughed at his rival.

At the foot of Burnt Mill Hill, Wilmot leapt down from the coach and stood waiting for Gallagher to arrive. Kennish drove a little way up the hill, but turned as Gallagher finally came level with Wilmot. It appeared that further words were exchanged but then Gallagher lashed out with the handle end of his whip. Wilmot paused for a moment, then staggered across the road to the far side where he fell on to a pile of rough stones. Both coaches now stopped and Gallagher and Kennish dashed back to where Wilmot lay.

Some other men gathered around and Gallagher asked them to assist him in carrying Wilmot's unconscious form to a nearby public house where Gallagher purchased a tot of brandy and forced it between Wilmot's lips. It had little effect and medical aid was called for. Gallagher, meanwhile, had returned to his coach and apparently set off to complete his journey to Ramsey.

In fact, Gallagher only continued as far as the Halfway House public house on the road to Laxey. Going inside he spoke to Jane Shimmin, the wife of the landlord, and asked if he might borrow a whip. Jane called her husband, John, and Gallagher told him that his whip had been broken. He also mentioned that he thought he had hurt a man back along the road.

Gallagher never did complete his journey to Ramsey. Deciding that he had better return to Douglas to face the authorities, he found that he was too late in that aim. The police had already been informed of what had happened on Burnt Mill Hill and Gallagher was arrested as he left Laxey for, by now, Wilmot had died – and much would be made of the fact that Gallagher had apparently disposed of his whip somewhere between Douglas and Laxey.

The inquest on the dead man opened that same day and a number of witnesses to the incident were called.

Thomas Quayle was at the foot of Burnt Mill Hill, filling his own cart with sand, when he saw the two coaches approach. After Wilmot had jumped down, he saw Gallagher transfer to the opposite seat on his own coach, so that he could be closer to Wilmot. He saw Gallagher lash out with the handle end of his whip but did not see if the blow actually landed or not. What he did see was Wilmot stagger towards him and say, 'You've seen that.' To which Gallagher had shouted, 'Keep out of the road then.' Wilmot had then fallen on to the stones at Quayle's feet, and there was blood on his face. Gallagher seemed genuinely concerned as he came over to the scene himself. He took a hand-kerchief and wiped some of the blood from Wilmot's face and helped to carry him into the public house.

William Kennish had also gone to where Wilmot lay and saw him being carried by Gallagher and others. He swore that, as they did so, he heard Gallagher say that he had hurt Wilmot with his whip.

Thomas Teare, who was fourteen, had been a guard on the coach driven by Kennish. He too had turned around in time to see the attack, but again could not swear that the blow had actually landed.

Hugh McKenna was also standing at the foot of the hill and saw the altercation, but again could not swear that Wilmot had actually been hit. Similar evidence was given by James Barber, who was coming down the hill, but he did state that after Gallagher had struck out, Wilmot had put his hand to his forehead.

Burnt Mill Hill in Douglas, now known as Summer Hill. This is where Edwin Wilmot met his death on 10 December 1864

Medical evidence was given by Dr Maxwell Fleming, who noted a slight wound, with some swelling, on the upper left side of Wilmot's head. There was another wound near the ear on the same side. He had performed the postmortem, assisted by Dr Ring and, though they had found a good deal of blood over the surface of the brain, there was no fracture to the skull.

The jury, having listened to the evidence, returned a verdict of wilful murder against Patrick Gallagher. In due course, a three-day court hearing felt that if Gallagher were responsible, he had not intended to kill Wilmot, and the charge was reduced to one of manslaughter.

Gallagher's defence were convinced that the best way to save their client was to establish a reasonable doubt in the collective minds of the jury as to what had actually caused Wilmot's death: the supposed blow from Gallagher's whip, or the subsequent fall upon the stones. They called on the assistance of a veritable team of doctors who, after carefully examining the evidence, came to the conclusion that Wilmot had been killed by the fall. They argued that if the whip handle had connected they would have expected a fracture of the skull and for Wilmot to be immediately rendered unconscious.

When Gallagher finally faced his trial, on Friday, 19 May 1865, in Castle Rushen, it was this evidence that swayed the jury. After a deliberation of one hour and twenty minutes, they returned to court to announce that Patrick Gallagher was not guilty.

The Murder of John Kermode – 1866

This story is covered in detail in Chapter 3.

James Killey – 1868

James Killey was a devoted father and a good husband to his wife of seven years, Esther. Employed as a labourer at the mines at Foxdale, he also farmed a few acres of land at Doarlish Ard. By all accounts James was a hard worker and a sober man, but this was to change in March 1868.

It was in that month that James finished work one day and, on his way home, called in at a public house in Glen Maye. No one could ever be sure what had happened, but from that day onwards James was a changed man. He became depressed, spoke rarely, and lost his appetite. He also began to make rambling statements, most of which were shown to be untrue. For example, on Wednesday, 1 April, he told his wife that he had lost his job at the mine, that the family were about to be evicted from their cottage, and that he wished them to go to America. In fact, he had not been dismissed, and there was no intention of evicting them from their home.

Things were not helped by a death in the family. On Friday, 3 April, James took three of his five children to view the body of a young nephew who had died and was due to be buried that afternoon. He took the girls to his mother's house where the body lay and, after returning home, told his wife that they had better get ready for the funeral, though it was not due to take place until some hours later. Soon afterwards, James wandered off into the fields and his wife, Esther, was so concerned for his well-being that she asked her brother, Archibald Shimmin, to go after him and make sure that he was all right. Later that same day, things would come to a terrible conclusion.

James returned to his cottage and seemed to be studying a well that stood in front of the property. At the time, four of his children were playing outside, around the well, and James could not have failed to notice them. He then went inside the house and destroyed some rather valuable family papers. Once again, Esther grew concerned and sent her eldest child, Emily, to get help from Archibald Shimmin.

Esther was inside the house, taking care of the baby, three-month-old Madeline, and saw James go out. Within minutes she heard a terrible scream and one of the girls crying 'Dadda!' Dashing outside, Esther saw that where there had been three children, there was now only one and James held that child and was about to hurl her down the well.

Still carrying the baby, Esther ran forward but it was too late. James threw his daughter down the well and then moved towards Esther. They then struggled as he tried to pull little Madeline from her arms. He proved to be too strong for her. He snatched the baby and threw her down into the gaping maw of the well. Esther managed to pull away from her husband and ran off down the road to get help just as the last daughter, Emily, returned. Turning back, Esther was in time to see her husband grab Emily and throw her down the well before hurling himself in after his children.

Esther found her brother working in the fields with another man, David Corkill. She blurted out what had happened and the two men ran back to the cottage. They both looked down into the well but could see nothing in the darkness. Bravely, Archibald Shimmin climbed on to the bucket and lowered himself down into the darkness.

The first person Archibald found was Emily, who seemed to be unhurt. Next he found Anna Louisa, who was dead, followed by Elizabeth Esther, who also appeared to be unharmed. Finally he found Madeline, the baby of the family, who was also dead. Two bodies remained in the well: James himself, and the eldest child, 7-year-old Selina Agnes. Their bodies would be recovered later. In all, four people had died: James Killey and three of his children, Selina Agnes, Anna Louisa and Madeline.

The inquest on the four bodies opened at the cottage the following day before Samuel Harris, the High Bailiff of Douglas. In fact, there were two inquests – the first on the bodies of the three children, and the second on James himself. Medical evidence showed that all three girls had died as a result of drowning and it was no surprise that the jury returned the verdict that they had been killed by their father while he had been temporarily insane. The inquest on James then opened and it was concluded that he had taken his own life while suffering from temporary insanity.

The next day, Sunday, 5 April 1868, all four bodies were buried in a large double grave. James Killey's coffin was the first to be placed into the ground, then those of his three daughters were placed at his side. It was estimated that at least two thousand people attended the ceremony.

Margaret Stewart – 1869

The marriage of Samuel and Margaret Stewart was not a happy one. Both were addicted to drink and Samuel often beat his wife while he was under the influence. The couple had three children, but only the youngest, a 5-year-old also named Samuel, lived with them. The three lived in a single-roomed hovel on the ground floor of a house in Back Strand Street, Douglas, and many times Margaret had to support the family by begging on the streets.

In early July 1869, while again under the influence of drink, Samuel senior was injured in an accident involving a horse. He had to be taken to hospital where he would stay for a number of weeks. Meanwhile, Margaret took the opportunity to sell every item of furniture they owned, in order to get money for more drink. By Saturday, 24 July, the only thing inside the Stewarts' room was a pile of straw on which mother and child had to sleep.

The house at Back Strand Street consisted of two rooms on each of three floors, giving a total of six family homes. In fact, the entire top floor was vacant and only four rooms were occupied. Living opposite the Stewarts was Patrick Maxwell and his family: a total of five people. Upstairs, directly above the Stewarts, lived Jane Goodwin and her five children, and opposite her lived Mary Kewley and her two daughters. In all, when fully occupied, seventeen people lived in those four rooms.

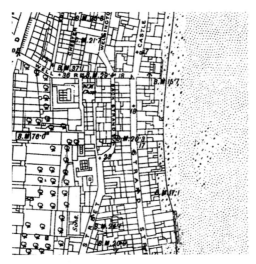

The area around Back
Strand Street, Douglas,
where Margaret
Stewart lived

Jane Goodwin was in and out of the house a few times on that Saturday and she saw Margaret Stewart and her son twice – once at 7 p.m. and once at 10.30 p.m. On both occasions Margaret appeared to be sober.

By 11 p.m., Margaret was in Patrick Maxwell's room, talking to him for a few minutes. She left soon afterwards, and some minutes later Patrick took to his bed. He would hear nothing to disturb him that night and was unaware that, at some time before midnight, Margaret Stewart had sneaked back into his room and stolen a shoemaker's knife that lay on the table.

By 12.15 a.m. on Sunday, 25 July, Jane Goodwin had also retired to bed. Soon afterwards she was disturbed by Margaret swearing in the room below. Fifteen minutes after this, Jane heard her son Samuel shout 'Oh Mamma, don't do that!' At first Jane Goodwin took no notice, but when the cry was repeated again a minute or so later, she shouted down to Margaret, telling her not to hurt the child.

Concerned for the safety of the child, Jane got up, dressed and went across to Mary Kewley's room, telling her what she had just heard. The two ladies then ventured downstairs and, looking through a hole in the wall of Margaret's room, saw to their horror that little Samuel was dead. His throat had been cut and there was a great deal of blood around his head. Of Margaret Stewart there was no sign.

In fact, Margaret had walked down to the seashore at Douglas, taking the shoemaker's knife with her. Daniel Ward, who lived in Strand Street but who was also on the seashore, looking after his boat, saw her approach but, when Margaret saw him, she turned her back on him.

Daniel saw Margaret moving her hand back and forth across her throat but could not see clearly what had happened. At this point, Daniel's daughter and son also appeared and it was his daughter who saw that Margaret had cut her own throat. At the same moment as Daniel's daughter was telling her father what had happened, Margaret rushed forward, throwing herself into the sea. It was with some difficulty that she was rescued.

The inquest on the dead child opened the following day, Monday, 26 July, and it did not take long for the jury to confirm that Samuel had been murdered by his mother. Margaret, however, never did face her trial. After initially showing good signs of recovery, she suffered a relapse and died on Sunday, 1 August. Her own inquest concluded that she had taken her own life while suffering temporary insanity.

William Edward Makepeace Williams – 1870

William Williams was a native of Solihull, but in June 1869 he moved to the Isle of Man and stayed at the Castle Mona Hotel in Douglas until January 1870. It was at the Castle Mona that he met Emma Caroline Goldthorpe who worked as a barmaid, and the two started seeing each other. An engagement was announced and, in February 1870, the couple married in Manchester and then honeymooned in Europe.

On 14 May 1870, the newlyweds returned to the Isle of Man with Emma's brother, William Goldthorpe, and booked into a guest house in Castle Terrace where, in a box on the mantelpiece in the sitting-room, lay a revolver.

It was a most curious weapon with two barrels and chambers, which could hold a total of twenty bullets. From the outset, William Williams was fascinated by the weapon and was often found looking at it.

On Thursday, 19 May, Williams, his wife and brother-in-law all took a trip to Laxey, stopping off along the way at a public house where Williams had a glass of beer, followed by a small bottle of claret. In due course, they set off back towards Douglas, with Emma and her brother in a small carriage while Williams rode a horse. At one stage, around 5 p.m., he galloped off, saying that he wanted to look at a house. Emma and her brother returned to their lodgings, only to find that Williams had not yet returned. Eventually, William Goldthorpe rode off to find his brother-in-law. The two met on the road and agreed to go for another drink together. It was now around 8 p.m.

Arriving back at the lodgings in Castle Terrace, the two men went into the sitting-room where Tom Smith, another guest, was relaxing. William Williams strolled purposefully up to the mantelpiece and took the revolver out of its box. The weapon was fully loaded and Williams now took careful aim at Smith who, not surprisingly, ran out of the room.

Williams now put the revolver back into its case, but within ten minutes had removed it again and put it into his coat pocket. Moments later he took it out of his pocket, aimed it at the wall, and fired a single shot. Goldthorpe remonstated with Williams and asked him to put the gun back into its box. Ignoring this, Williams simply opened a window and proceeded to fire the remaining nineteen shots into Castle Mona Road. Fortunately, no one was injured.

Goldthorpe tried in vain to get the gun from Williams, but he would have none of it. He reloaded at least some of the chambers and announced that he was going out. Goldthorpe thought it would be prudent to go with his brother-in-law, to make sure that he did not get into any trouble.

The area in Douglas where William Williams was staying and where he fired the gun into Castle Mona Road

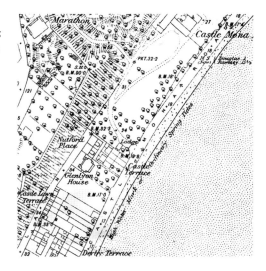

By 10 p.m., the two men were in Trustrum's Hotel in James Street but they did not stay there very long. Goldthorpe was no doubt relieved as they strolled back towards the lodging house, along Strand Street, but as they turned into Castle Street they walked past the Derby Arms Hotel and Williams said he wanted to go in for a drink.

It was 10.30 p.m. as Goldthorpe and Williams entered the Derby Arms and ordered two sherries. Williams then drew the revolver out again, causing the barmaid, Margaret Anne Cannell, to run from the room in order to find the landlord, John Gold, and tell him that there was a man with a gun in the bar.

John Gold entered the bar and stood behind the counter, intending to keep an eye on this possibly troublesome customer. Williams had been in the bar a number of times before so Gold engaged him in conversation, but at one stage Williams shouted, 'I am a good shot and would like to blow through your hat.' He then pointed the revolver directly at Gold's head, squeezed the trigger, and fired a single round. Gold fell to the ground, his hat still on his head, as Goldthorpe half-dragged Williams from the bar.

William Williams seemed oblivious to what he had just done. Ignoring Goldthorpe's cries that he had just shot and killed a man, Williams said that this was nonsense and Gold wasn't hurt. Finally, Goldthorpe got his brother-in-law back to the lodging house. Williams immediately retired to his room while Goldthorpe told Emma what had just happened.

A shot rang out and, dashing into the bedroom, Emma and Goldthorpe found Williams lying on his bed, having shot himself in the forehead. He was still alive and medical assistance was summoned.

In fact, two doctors attended two patients at almost the same time. Dr James Jackson Adair went to the guest house where he began to treat Williams, but it was all to no avail and Williams died within minutes of the doctor's arrival. Maenwhile, Dr Thomas Arthur Wood had gone to the Derby Arms where he found Gold unconscious but still alive. He noted a single wound in the crown of Gold's head, which penetrated down into the brain. He was also unable to save his patient and Gold died soon afterwards.

The inquest on both men opened on Friday, 20 May. After the medical evidence had been given, a tearful Emma Williams informed the court that her husband had always been given to somewhat strange behaviour, especially when he had taken alcoholic drink. She also said that even a small quantity of such drink could affect him rather badly, though at all other times he was most kind and attentive.

The proceedings were soon over and the jury reached the expected verdicts: Gold had been killed by Williams, who had then taken his own life; and both acts had been committed while Williams was suffering from temporary insanity.

John Kewish – 1872

This story is covered in detail in Chapter 4.

Sarah Lewin – 1875

Alcohol was a problem for Charles and Sarah Lewin of Queen Street, Castletown. They were both heavy drinkers and often argued when under the influence. Indeed, by 1875, all the neighbours knew that they simply did not get on.

On Friday, 24 December, yet another argument led to Sarah going across to Catherine Teare's house at 2 a.m. She stayed for less than an hour before returning to the marital bed.

After rising at 9 a.m., Sarah Lewin spent a good deal of time going from one neighbour's house to another. First she went to her brother's house and then went back to Catherine Teare's where she stayed until around 5 p.m. She returned briefly to her own house to find her husband asleep. Sarah didn't actually see him, but it was clear from the deep snoring from the bedroom that this is what Charles was doing.

After going out again, Sarah was back home at 8.30 p.m. Charles was now apparently lying asleep on the hallway floor, something that had happened before if he had had too much to drink. Again she did not stay out long, but was back home for one final visit some time after 11 p.m., when she found that Charles was still lying in the hallway. By 4 a.m., Sarah was at Elizabeth Harper's house where she had to be helped to bed, being the worse for drink.

At 10 a.m. on Christmas Day, John Taubman was passing Charles Lewin's house when he heard what sounded like a low moan coming from within. Finding the door unlocked, Taubman pushed it open and found Charles still lying on the hallway floor. He was unconscious and there was a lot of blood about. Further, three objects lay near the body: a fork, a small poker and a large stone. Taubman then ran to William Gelling's house for assistance. The doctor was summoned and he ordered that Charles be taken up to his bed. It was there that he died, at 3 p.m. that afternoon.

The inquest opened on 26 December and various witnesses

were called to detail the movements of both Charles and Sarah Lewin.

Charles had been seen in New Street, at 7 p.m. on 24 December, by George Karran, who described him as rolling about a good deal, having apparently had a few drinks. The testimony did not, however, agree with that of three other witnesses. Wayne Carroll had seen Charles in the marketplace and said he was sober at the time. Later still, at 9 p.m., William Clucas had seen him in Arbory Street and agreed that Charles was sober. Finally, Elizabeth Carr had seen Charles at 10.30 p.m., apparently making his way home, and she too said that he was sober at this time.

Sarah Lewin's testimony as to her movements was confirmed by a number of witnesses. At 5 p.m. she had been in Elizabeth Harper's house where she stayed until 7.45 p.m. From there she went for a drink with James Kelly, and at 8.30 p.m., returned home to find Charles lying on the floor in the hallway. In fact, she hadn't actually seen Charles clearly as it was very dark and so had not noticed if he was injured in any way.

From there, Sarah had gone to Letitia Taubman's house and then back to Mrs Harper's, staying there until 11 p.m. After a brief visit to her own home, she spent fifteen minutes or so at Catherine Teare's house before returning yet again to Elizabeth Harper's where she stayed until 2 a.m. Then, after going out to the Liverpool Arms, she returned to Elizabeth Harper's home at around 3 a.m. Finally, at 4 a.m., she had gone up to bed, assisted by Elizabeth and Ann Carphey.

The inquest verdict was that Charles Lewin had died as a result of violence from some person or persons unknown. In short, he had been murdered. On Monday, 10 January, Sarah had been arrested on suspicion of murder and she was formally charged on Thursday, 13 January.

Less than two weeks later, on 25 January, Sarah appeared in court, defended by Mr Laughton who said that there was not sufficient evidence to send Sarah for trial and the facts of the case were such that Charles may well have died due to falling downstairs. The magistrates deliberated the arguments for twenty minutes before agreeing with that conclusion and Sarah was released from custody. No other arrest was ever made in connection with the death of Charles Lewin.

The Murder of Elizabeth Crowe – 1888

On Friday, 21 December 1888, William Goldsmith was on his way to work at the quarry at Ballure. It was around 7 a.m. and as he strolled up Old Douglas Road he found a body lying at the side of the narrow trackway. It was very dark and William could not even tell if the body was that of a man or a woman, but he could see that there was a good deal of blood on the face. He turned towards Ramsey, intending to report the matter to the police.

William had not gone far when he met James Corkill. He told James what he had found and Corkill said he would go to get help while William returned to where the body lay. By 7.30 a.m., Corkill had taken Constable William Caley to the scene, and by that time William Goldsmith had recognized the body as that of Elizabeth Crowe, a spinster, who lived further up the lane in a cottage named Dreemlang.

Elizabeth Crowe was well known in the area. She kept a couple of cows and earned a living for herself by selling their milk in and around Ramsey. She normally travelled into the town daily and police investigations soon showed that she had done so the previous day, Thursday, 20 December.

Further inquiries revealed that Elizabeth had called at James Duffy's house in Back Lane at around 7.55 p.m. that evening, and later she had called at William Caine's house where she had something to eat, staying there until around 10.45 p.m. She was last seen by two men, Robert Edward Corlett and Thomas Rawcliffe, who had left the Queen's Hotel in Ramsey at 11 p.m. They had walked with Elizabeth as far as the Old Douglas Road. As she turned off up the roadway, they walked on a little and waited for two friends. This information put the likely time of the attack on Elizabeth at some minutes after 11 p.m.

On the same day that the body was discovered, the inquest opened before Samuel Harris, the coroner for Douglas. The first witness was Dr John Gell who had been called to the scene by the police. He counted a number of wounds on Elizabeth's head and there were signs that the body had been dragged along the lane to the spot where it was finally discovered.

Constable Caley had made a search of the immediate area and had found blood on a number of stones. Further, one stone also had some hair adhering to it and this was believed to be the murder weapon. The inquest was then adjourned until the following Thursday.

Meanwhile, a possible suspect had come to the attention of the police. It was common knowledge in the area that Elizabeth Crowe did not get on with her neighbours, the Gelling family, who lived in a cottage further up Old Douglas Road. Indeed, a year or so before, Elizabeth had accused Catherine Gelling and her son John of assault. The case had finally been dismissed, but there was certainly bad blood between the two families.

As a result of this information, the police called on the Gellings early on the morning of Saturday, 22 December. The house was searched and a blue coat found that was still wet, appearing to have been washed or soaked in water. This, and other evidence, led to John Gelling being arrested on suspicion of murder. He made his first court appearance on Monday, 24 December, when he was remanded to the gaol at Castle Rushen.

The inquest reopened after Christmas, on Thursday, 27 December, and continued into the following week. By now, Dr Gell had performed a postmorten and had confirmed that Elizabeth had died as a result of a fracture of the base of the skull. He was followed to the stand by Constable Caley, who gave details of the previous animosity and arguments between Elizabeth and the Gellings.

Evidence was also given on the movements of the man accused of Elizabeth's murder, John Gelling. Gelling stated that he had been at home until 9 p.m. on Thursday, 20 December. He had walked into Ramsey, but not down the Old Douglas Road as that was rather muddy and dirty. On the way he had called at Kewey Kneal's house to drop off a rope, leaving there at around 9.30 p.m.

Arriving in Ramsey, he had met a friend named Peckham who he spent some time with before going to William Skillicorn's house where he stayed until just before midnight. He then returned home, but again did not go up Old Douglas Road, finally arriving home at around 12.45 a.m. on 21 December. As for the blue coat that had been found at his house, Gelling admitted he had sponged down one of the pockets as he had let some toffee melt and it had stained the coat at that point.

Much of this testimony was indeed confirmed. William Skillicorn stated that Gelling had been at his house and left around midnight.

John Corlett had been at Gelling's house, arriving there at about 10.20 p.m. on 20 December. He was still there when John Gelling came home at approximately 12.45 a.m. the next morning, and he recalled that Gelling's mother remonstrated with him for coming home so late.

The jury retired on Wednesday, 2 January, and when they returned to court announced that Elizabeth Crowe had been wilfully murdered and there was 'strong suspicion' attached to John Gelling.

Gelling made his appearance in court on Monday, 7 January, when all the evidence was heard again and he was then ordered to be sent for trial on the charge of murder. The evidence, though, was purely circumstantial and the case rather weak. As a result, when Gelling's trial opened, on Monday, 18 February 1889, before Deemster Gill, the prosecution chose not to put any evidence before the jury and Gelling was duly discharged. The case remains unsolved.

William Kelly – 1889

William Kelly was a good husband and father. A plasterer by trade, he and his wife, Margaret Elizabeth Nicholson Kelly, had had thirteen children in all, though seven of these had died. By 1889, only three children remained at home: Charles, Louis, and the youngest daughter, 16-year-old Christina.

The family lived in two rooms in James Street, Douglas, and, though he was a most even-tempered man, William was known to like a drink. Once he had partaken of alcohol he could become rather argumentative, but no one ever described him as a violent man.

In November 1889, another member of the Kelly brood was actually staying at James Street. Isabella Tyman, a married daughter, was staying with her parents while her husband was at sea. On Tuesday, 26 November, a neighbour, Thomas William Corlett, called on the family at around 7.40 a.m. He stayed for around four hours, during which time William Kelly went out a couple of times to get what he described as a 'noggin of rum'. Although it was plain that he had been drinking, he was still in an amiable enough mood.

At 11.40 a.m. Margaret and her daughter, Christina, were preparing lunch and Corlett was invited to stay. He declined politely and left the house with Christina. They walked down one flight of stairs and stood talking for a few minutes. Isabella, meanwhile, was in the room upstairs. Suddenly a cry rang out. William Kelly shouted, 'Bella. Come, I have murdered your mother.'

Corlett and Christina dashed back upstairs to find Margaret Kelly sitting in an armchair, her head thrown back and a large gash in her throat. There was a large amount of blood and both Christina and Isabella, who had by now gone

Broadway where Elizabeth Galsworthy stayed at the time of her death

downstairs, tried to staunch the wound with cloths while Corlett ran for help. He returned with Dr Woods and Police Constable Corkish.

Margaret was beyond all aid and Dr Woods certified that she was dead. William Kelly readily repeated that he was responsible for her death, claiming that he had been provoked. He was taken into custody and charged with murder.

The inquest opened the same day that Margaret died. Jane Loughlin, a neighbour, said that she had heard the couple exchanging words the previous night. This was, in part, confirmed by Christina, but she added that Margaret and William had been very good parents. Unfortunately, her mother did aggravate her father, often using harsh language to him. She also made accusations of some terrible behaviour on her father's part, none of which was true.

Dr Black had attended the house where Margaret died and he reported that she was dead by the time he arrived. Margaret's throat had been cut and her windpipe severed. The artery on the right side of her neck had also been cut and blood had spurted a distance of approximately 9 feet.

Superintendent Fayle, who had been in charge of the case, said that William Kelly had consistently admitted that he had killed his wife. He claimed that she had accused him of having affairs with other women and even of being involved with Christina, his daughter. During this argument she had sat down in the chair, thrown her head back to reveal her neck and taunted him, daring him to cut her throat. He had simply lost control and done so, instantly regretting his actions.

The jury verdict, when it came, was that William Kelly was responsible for his wife's death, but that he had acted under considerable provocation. Just over a week later, on Friday, 6 December, Kelly appeared before Deemster Drinkwater where, the evidence having been heard, it was decided to send him for trial on a charge of manslaughter, not murder.

Kelly's trial took place on Friday, 17 January 1890, where he pleaded guilty to the charge. He was sentenced to ten years' imprisonment.

George Cooper – 1892

This story is covered in detail in Chapter 5.

Alfred Kelly and Ellis Corlett – 1899

Elizabeth Galsworthy was a woman of property and wealth, who lived in Leeds. Her husband had died in 1898 and left her well provided for, but there was one problem: Elizabeth liked a drink, though she did her best to conceal this from the people who knew her.

In August 1899, Elizabeth decided that she would take a holiday on the Isle of Man and so, on Saturday, 26 August, travelled to the island with William Thorpe Pearson who acted as a form of agent for her. Pearson's wife and two children accompanied them and the party of five booked into a guest house at 10 Broadway, run by Betty Knowles. The group stayed there until 4 September when the Pearsons returned to Leeds. Elizabeth stayed on at the guest house and continued her holiday.

William Franklin was the landlord of the Old Strand Inn, situated in Strand Street, Douglas, but had moved there from Leeds where he had been a neighbour of Elizabeth Galsworthy. The two knew each other very well and Elizabeth was in the habit of calling in at William's establishment on an almost daily basis. Sometimes this would be simply to exchange the time of day and enjoy a cup of tea, but occasionally she would sit down with William for a meal. The last time William saw Elizabeth was on Friday, 22 September, when she informed him that she didn't feel too well and took a small bottle of gin with her when she left.

The very next day, Saturday, 23 September, Elizabeth visited the Central Hotel bar, also in Broadway, where she ordered a glass of whisky and milk. She left soon afterwards but returned to the bar at 1.15 p.m. when she ordered another whisky and milk. She took this into the sitting-room where she fell into conversation with two cab drivers: Ellis Corlett and Alfred Kelly.

John Burton, the head barman, was working at the hotel that afternoon and later served Elizabeth with a gin and milk, a small whisky and a glass of beer. Apparently Elizabeth was now purchasing drinks for her new-found friends. Indeed, Burton could not but help overhear their conversation and their agreement to go for a drive together.

That afternoon and evening, all three travelled around the area, calling at various public houses. They visisted Crebbin's Hotel, the Groudle Hotel, the Liverpool Arms Hotel, the Prince of Wales in Onchan, and the Bowling Green which was close to Derby Square. It was there that the three met up with William Christian, another cab driver. By now, Alfred Kelly had had enough and announced that he was going back to his lodgings. Elizabeth and Corlett expressed the desire to go on to the Quarter Bridge Inn and Christian offered to drive them.

Several more drinks were consumed and, in due course, William Christian tried to get them both to go home. Elizabeth and Corlett refused and now Corlett himself took over the driving of the horse-drawn cab.

Eventually, Corlett took the cab back to the stables in Derby Square and made his weary way back to the lodgings he shared with Joseph Martin. Martin was still awake and noticed that it was some time between 1 a.m. and 2 a.m. on Sunday, 24 September.

The stables were owned by William Clague who was Corlett's employer. At 9.30 a.m. on that same Sunday, Corlett called at Clague's house and informed him that there was a woman lying dead in one of the stables. Clague told Corlett to fetch the police while he went to see for himself.

Sure enough, there was a woman's body in the hay. She lay on her back with her hat and umbrella near her head. Police Sergeant McLaughlin was soon in attendance and, upon making a more careful examination, found that the woman's undergarments were saturated with blood. The unfortunate woman was soon identified as Elizabeth Galsworthy and, once stories of the previous evening's drinking spree came to McLaughlin's attention, both Ellis Corlett and Alfred Kelly were arrested on suspicion of murder.

The inquest opened on Monday, 25 September, before Samuel Harris, the coroner for Douglas. Dr T. A. MacKenzie had been called to the scene by the police and he had determined that the large quantity of blood found had issued from the woman's vagina.

On the second day, witnesses were called to testify to Elizabeth's drinking habits. So, for example, James Quinn, a barman at the Central Hotel, confirmed that Elizabeth had come into the bar every day, at around lunchtime. Other witnesses from the various public houses that Elizabeth, Corlett and Kelly had visited were called to establish the timetable and to confirm that they all seemed to be rather the worse for drink. Indeed, in some establishments, the landlords had refused to serve them, believing that they had already had more than enough to drink.

It had been suggested that the injury to Elizabeth's vagina might well have been caused during rough sexual intercourse. Initially both Kelly and Corlett denied any such intimate contact with Elizabeth, but tests had now shown that blood had also been found on Corlett's trousers, though none had been found on Kelly's clothing. Corlett now admitted that he had been intimate with Elizabeth, but it had been consensual and had happened close to the Quarter Bridge Inn. Later, he had driven the cab back to Derby Square, but it was now much too late for Elizabeth to return to her lodgings so Corlett told her she would have to sleep on the hay. She had made no complaint to him about feeling ill or being injured.

The jury retired to consider their verdict. When they returned to court, the verdict was that Elizabeth's death had been due to the haemorrhage and that Ellis Corlett was to blame.

Alfred Kelly may well have thought that this ordeal was now over for him. He had left the group long before Elizabeth had received her injury and no blood had been found on his clothing. However, no sooner was the inquest verdict announced than Kelly and Corlett were both arrested and charged with murder.

The first court appearance was on Thursday, 28 September, before the High Bailiff of Douglas, Mr J. M. Cruickshank. The same witnesses were called over the two-day hearing where it was decided that Kelly had no case to answer and, finally, he was discharged. Corlett was sent for trial.

In fact, Corlett never did face his trial for murder. On Saturday, 21 October, he made another appearance in court where it was announced that there was really no case against him. He too was discharged, but not before being rebuked for having left Elizabeth in such a state.

Summary

Name	Year	Crime	Final Sentence
James Kewley	1859	Murder	Escaped prosecution
Patrick Gallagher	1864	Murder	Not guilty
John Kermode	1866	Murder	Unsolved
James Killey	1868	Murder	Committed suicide
Margaret Stewart	1869	Murder	Committed suicide
William Williams	1870	Murder	Committed suicide
John Kewish	1872	Murder	Executed
Sarah Lewin	1875	Murder	Not prosecuted
John Gelling	1888	Murder	Not guilty
William Kelly	1889	Manslaughter	Ten years
George Cooper	1892	Manslaughter	Ten years
Ellis Corlett	1899	Murder	Not prosecuted
Alfred Kelly	1899	Murder	Not prosecuted

7

Feeding the Rabbits

Catherine Elizabeth Quayle was becoming concerned. It was getting quite late on the morning of Monday, 27 April 1914, and her namesake, Mrs Quayle, who ran the grocery opposite, still hadn't opened up for business.

Catherine ran a sweetshop from 43 Bucks Road, Douglas, and had last seen Frances Alice Quayle, who was no relation, at around 10.20 p.m. on the previous Saturday, 25 April, when she had called into the shop to buy herself some sweets. The two women had a brief conversation and Frances had told her that she was on her way to her garden to feed the rabbits she kept there.

As the hours passed, Catherine grew increasingly worried about Frances, and decided to take her concerns to a neighbour, John Kelly, a carman who also had premises in Bucks Road. Together, they then went across to the grocery shop and noted that the blinds were still down. Investigating further, Catherine found that the side door to the premises was closed, but unlocked, so she and Kelly now ventured inside, calling out for Mrs Quayle. There was no reply, the gas was still burning in the kitchen, and the sweets that the missing woman had purchased on the Saturday lay untouched on the table. Without further delay, John Kelly returned to his own premises and telephoned Mr Cowley, Mrs Quayle's son-in-law, who lived at 2 Selborn Road.

In due course, John Cowley arrived at Bucks Road and, together with Mr Kelly, went to inspect the shop. Sure enough, there was no sign of Mrs Quayle, but there was a possible solution to this mystery.

*43 Bucks Road from where
Frances Alice Quayle ran her
grocery business*

Frances Alice Quayle was a woman of habit. Every night she would lock up her shop at the close of business and, no matter how late it was, would then walk to her allotment to feed some rabbits she kept there. Indeed, on the night she was last seen alive, Frances had told Catherine Quayle, the sweet-shop owner, that this is what she was about to do. Perhaps, they thought, having carried out this task the previous evening, she had fallen ill there. It was certainly worth checking out.

The allotments were at the back of Finch Hill Church in Tynwald Street, but the door that led to them was actually in a lane that ran behind Tynwald Street School and which was known as Finch Hill Grove. Cowley and Kelly found, to their dismay, that the door to the allotments was locked and they did not have a key. Undaunted, John Cowley then took a walk up to the bridge nearby as this would give him a view down into the gardens. It was from that vantage point that he could see the body of a woman, slumped in a sitting position, between a greenhouse and a shed.

It was clearly time to gain entrance to the gardens and,

returning to where Kelly waited, Cowley reported what he had seen. He was then helped up on to the top of the wall and jumped down into the gardens. Having made his way to where the body lay, Cowley then waited with his mother-in-law while Kelly ran for help.

It was obvious to Cowley that Frances had been subjected to some sort of attack as there was a good deal of blood about and the poor lady had suffered severe head injuries. Seeing that there was, apparently, no key either in the lock, or close by Frances's body, Cowley grabbed a spade and smashed the lock off the door. Now, at least, when help arrived they would have no difficulty getting in to the gardens.

John Kelly had run for Dr T.A. MacKenzie, but he was out of the district so his assistant, Dr Henry Caird, accompanied Kelly back to the allotment. Caird noted that the body lay huddled in a short passageway between a greenhouse and shed, along one wall of which were a number of rabbit hutches. It appeared that Frances had been in the process of feeding the rabbits when an assailant had come up behind her and struck her with such severity that her head had completely caved in. Her face was covered in blood and her brain protruded from the wound. Indeed, blood and brain matter had been splashed up the wall of the shed to a distance of around 6 feet. Dr Caird pronounced life 'extinct' and ordered that the police be summoned immediately.

It wasn't long before Superintendent Quillann and Detective Constable Hayle had arrived. Investigations revealed that some of the occupants of the houses in Fairfield Terrace and the other cottages around the gardens claimed that they had heard a single scream at around 11 p.m. on the Saturday. Had it been Frances Quayle calling for help?

A search of the shop premises showed that apparently nothing had been stolen, though it should be remembered that Frances's keys were missing and one of the doors to her shop had been left open. Had the killer stolen those keys with a view to gaining access to the shop and then either changed their mind, or found nothing to tempt them on the premises? In fact, those missing keys were very soon traced.

Mary Jane Canida, along with her family, had been on her way to church at 7.30 a.m. on the Sunday. As they walked, her young son found a bunch of keys behind a shop owned by Mr Parkes, near Princes Street. The keys appeared to be stained with blood so Mary ordered her son to put them back where he had found them and later reported the matter to a constable. This officer had then gone to the spot indicated and retrieved the keys. The officer had called on a number of premises in the area, trying to trace the owner, and had finally taken the keys to the police station. Now, when these were checked, one was found to open the door to the gardens where the murder had taken place, and the rest fitted the shop doors. This indicated that the attack had probably taken place late on the Saturday night after Frances Quayle had closed her shop, and linked in with the cry heard at 11 p.m.

The inquest on Frances Quayle opened at 11 a.m. on Tuesday, 28 April, before the High Bailiff of Douglas. At the start of the proceedings the jury were taken to view the body and then escorted to the scene of the crime. After this, formal evidence of identification was given by John Cowley. He explained that Mrs Quayle had been a widow, aged about fifty-five, her husband Thomas Henry Quayle having died some thirty years before. The couple had had just one child, a daughter, Maud, who was of course married to the witness.

Continuing his testimony, Cowley explained that Frances had lived alone in her shop at 40 Bucks Road. Her father, William Cubbon, had died some nine years before when he fell off the cliffs at Douglas Head. Finally, Frances had two brothers, one of whom lived in Ballaugh, while the other had emigrated to Australia. After this information had been given, the inquest was adjourned until 11 a.m. on 5 May, to give the police time to make their enquiries.

On the evening of the same day that the inquest had been opened, two detectives from Scotland Yard, Detective Chief

Inspector Ward and Detective Sergeant Cooper, arrived on the island to assist the police. A number of well-known local characters were picked up for questioning, but all were soon released without any charges being brought.

What had initially promised to be an interesting lead proved to be nothing of the kind when a nurse from the hospital reported that she had seen two men and a youth running from the direction of Tynwald Street during the early hours of Sunday morning. The three individuals were traced, and shown to have a perfectly innocent reason for being out and about at that early hour.

On Thursday, 30 April, the body of Frances Quayle was laid to rest in the cemetery at Braddan. That same day, her son-in-law, John Cowley, offered a £50 reward for anyone with information that might lead to an arrest.

By now, some witnesses had come forward who reported seeing Frances on the Saturday night and their testimony gave the police a more accurate idea of what had taken place.

Albert Skillicorn worked as an errand boy for the murdered woman and he reported that he had left the shop at 10.15 p.m. by which time Mrs Quayle had locked up for the night. The boy also reported that earlier that evening, at around 9 p.m., he had been sent with a message to Mr Kneale in Peveril Street. As he was returning to the shop, Albert passed down Tynwald Street where he saw a man standing against the wall, close by the gardens. The man appeared to be drunk.

Joseph Bucknall had gone to the sweetshop between 10.30 p.m. and 10.35 p.m. and, just as he was entering, Frances Quayle was leaving with the sweets she had purchased. Since the sweets were later found on Frances's table, it was obvious that she had returned home first before walking down to her gardens and it appears she was next seen at some time just after 10.40 p.m.

Thomas Cremnell had been to the Strand Cinema on the Saturday evening and left there at about 10.15 p.m. He went straight home but then, ten minutes later, decided to visit the sweetshop. On his way there he saw Frances Quayle in Princes Street. She was just entering the lane that led to the gardens and had a basket under her arm. She was alone and Cremnell did not see anyone else about.

Alice Dobson was on her way to a chip shop in Tynwald Street at around 11 p.m. and she saw Frances Quayle cross Tynwald Street and go up towards the door that led to the gardens. Alice did not see anyone else in the lane.

These two witnesses seemed to confirm that at some time between, say, 10.45 p.m. and 11 p.m., Frances Quayle was arriving at the garden where she would meet her death. However, the evidence of three other men indicated something a little different.

Ridgeway Quirk confirmed that he had seen Frances at about 10.45 p.m. at the bottom of Finch Hill Lane. She walked up the lane towards the garden and, since he was walking the same way, he was in effect following her a few steps behind. As he continued on his way, Quirk believed that he heard Frances actually unlock the door, close it behind her, and lock it again. He passed back down the lane soon afterwards and heard nothing. If Quirk's testimony was accurate, why had he not been seen by either Thomas Cremnell or Alice Dobson?

Then there was the evidence of James Bridson and his brother Alfred. They both walked down the lane at about 10.20 p.m. and saw the shadow of someone near the door to the gardens. Neither man could say whether this was a man or a woman, but as the brothers passed the doorway they both thought they heard the jingling of a bunch of keys, the door being opened and closed, and then locked on the inside. If this had been Frances Quayle letting herself in, then the times were wrong and, of course, they should have also been seen by other witnesses.

The testimony given by all of these witnesses again narrowed down the probable time of the attack to some time that night, probably close to 11 p.m., the time a single scream had been heard. Meanwhile, a more detailed report on

Frances's injuries had been prepared. It appeared that Frances may well have tried to defend herself as two fingers on her right hand were broken, as was one on her left. As stated earlier, the top of her head had been smashed in and her brain exposed.

The scene of the crime had been mapped out and photographed by the police. Upon entering the allotment through the door, the shed was to the immediate left. It was about 10 feet long and, at the end, a passageway – some 6 feet long – separated it from a small greenhouse. On the left side of this passageway – up against the shed wall – were the rabbit hutches, and it had been here that Frances had been attacked.

A large pool of blood lay at the top of the passage but the body had been moved from that spot to where it was finally found, in a sitting position. John Cowley had testified that he had moved Frances's body slightly, to see if he could offer any aid. Later still, he, Kelly and Dr Caird had lifted the body into the shed.

The investigation continued, and soon another piece of possible evidence was discovered. On a piece of waste ground, between Princes Street and Tynwald Street, a swivel or eye-bolt was discovered by Constable Philip Watterson as he searched the area. This was a tool, 13 inches long and almost 3 inches wide, and was used for tightening the wire supports on telegraph poles; the head of this eye-bolt was covered in blood. There were also human hairs adhering to the eye-bolt and subsequent tests showed that this blood and hair belonged to the victim. Clearly, the murder weapon had been discovered.

On 5 May, the inquest was adjourned again and the evidence was only finally detailed on Friday, 22 May. On that date, all the witnesses mentioned above were heard, but another – very curious – piece of information was also outlined.

This information came from Thomas Hall, a butcher's assistant living in Tynwald Street. He stated that at about 11 p.m. on the Saturday he had gone to Corlett's butcher shop in Bucks Road to buy some meat. As he walked home, Thomas encountered a local well-known vagrant, Thomas Angus Moore, who asked him what he had in his parcel. Hall replied that it was meat, whereupon Moore asked him for some. Hall refused, but did give the man a chew of tobacco.

As the two men were talking, Frances Quayle walked up the lane and Moore asked her if she was going to feed her rabbits. She confirmed that she was, at which point Moore asked her for a match. Frances handed one over and asked Hall if he would like some too. After he had taken a few, Mrs Quayle headed off towards her garden. At this, Moore picked up an eye-bolt lying on the ground and said, 'I have a mind to knock her brains out for refusing me tonight.' Then, as Hall walked off towards his home, Moore began to follow Mrs Quayle. Hall's last piece of testimony was that during these events, Moore's wife had also walked past them.

Hall had first told this story to Constable Bridson on Saturday, 2 May, and had then been interviewed by the two detectives from Scotland Yard. The story was, of course, checked and it was soon discovered that Moore could not possibly be the killer. At 10.45 p.m. that Saturday, Moore and his wife had been seen in Rose Mount by no less a witness than a police constable. Further, at 11.24 p.m., Moore was seen in Somerset Road. Local refuse collectors were just about to start work and Moore, for some reason, began abusing them. They, naturally, returned the insults. Finally, soon after this, Moore was seen again, this time near the Woodbourne Hotel. In short, Hall was simply not telling the truth.

Was Hall merely some kind of fantasist? Neighbours swore that he wasn't the kind of person to invent such a story, but his testimony was obviously mistaken and bore no resemblance to what other witnesses had said. There is, however, one final point.

By 5 May, which was three days after Hall had first told his story, the medical evidence showed that in all probability Frances Quayle had first been attacked while she was in a stooping position, possibly as she unfastened the rabbit hutch.

The first blow, to the back of her head, had been given with such force that the pin fastening the hutch had been driven through her face. She then fell to the ground and further blows were then rained upon her. It was also now reported that a broken box of matches had been found close by her body and Hall had claimed that Moore had asked her for a match, when he told his story. Could it be that Hall was merely seeking some publicity for himself? Alternatively, was he seeking to claim the £50 reward put up by John Cowley? Neither of those scenarios are compatible with Hall not being the kind of person to make stories up. Could it be that he was possibly involved in some other way? Could Hall himself have been responsible for Frances Quayle's death?

Whatever the truth, on 8 May the two detectives from Scotland Yard left the island, their enquiries exhausted. The inquest, on 22 May, returned the expected verdict of 'Wilful murder by person or persons unknown' and the case was left unsolved. It remains so to this day.

8

The Intruder

On Monday, 13 October 1930, Percy William Brooke decided that he wanted to spend some time shooting in the countryside around Snaefell. He climbed on to his bicycle at his home in Churchtown, Lezayre, and cycled to Lhergyrhenny Cottage, in Sulby Glen, about one mile from Tholt-y-Will, a cottage he also owned and where he kept his guns and ammunition.

As soon as he arrived at the cottage, Percy knew that something was wrong. He found that his key would not turn in the lock and there was a pane of glass broken in one of the windows. Percy had already heard that a stranger had been seen in the area the previous day, and he started to think that someone might well have broken in. He decided to seek help and walked to a field nearby where he had seen William Kinrade trapping rabbits.

Explaining to Kinrade that he believed someone had broken into his cottage, Percy asked him to go back with him. Kinrade agreed and the two men walked back to the cottage. By now it was some time after noon.

Percy entered the cottage through the broken window and opened the front door to let Kinrade in. As he did so, he saw that someone had put a piece of wire into the lock, which was why his key had not worked. Gingerly, the two men now crept further into the cottage. They went first into the kitchen, which had been ransacked. Looking more closely, Percy saw that his shotgun had been taken from its usual position, and at the same moment appeared to hear something upstairs – though Kinrade would later say that he had heard nothing.

The two men walked to the foot of a short flight of stairs and Percy called out 'Who's there?' There was no reply.

In fact, the stairs to the upper part of the cottage were split into two. Five steps led up to a small landing, and the stairs then turned through 90 degrees and continued up. Percy now began to walk slowly up those first five steps with Kinrade some way behind him.

As Percy reached the small landing, a single shot rang out from somewhere further up the stairs. To his horror, Kinrade saw Percy fall backwards, at his feet. He wasn't moving and Kinrade was sure that he was dead. Without any further delay, and in fear of his life, Kinrade ran from the house in order to get help.

Kinrade was lame so it took a little time before he found a group of men working on the roadway. William Christian, a tenant of Percy Brooke's, was also there and he ordered the men to the cottage while one of them, Ernest Fargher, took Kinrade to the police station at Ramsey.

It was some time later that Sergeant George W. Corkill, Constable Lancaster, Dr Kitchen and Kinrade himself reached the isolated cottage. William Christian and his workmen had surrounded Lhergyrhenny Cottage and confirmed that no one had left since their arrival. The police knew, of course, that the man, whoever he was, had a gun and had already used it. For that reason, they fired their own guns at the cottage putting two bullets through the kitchen window and three more through the upper windows of the property. No shots were returned and so, with great care, they moved forward into the cottage.

Percy Brooke still lay where he had fallen and Dr Kitchen confirmed that he was dead. A search of the rest of the cottage revealed that the assailant had flown, presumably before Christian and his men had arrived. It wasn't long, however, until a suspect was named.

Dr Skene had also, by now, attended the scene but his only connection with this shooting was his concern for someone who had escaped from his care: Thomas Edward Kissack, forty-five, had escaped from Bellamona Hospital, an asylum near Douglas, on Saturday, 11 October, two days before Percy Brooke had been shot.

Kissack was well known to the authorities. He had first been convicted of theft back in 1905 and further brushes with the law followed up until 1916, when he joined the army. This did nothing to curb his criminal tendencies, though, and in 1918 he was sentenced to two years' imprisonment, for theft, at Lewes in Sussex. It was here that his mental problems were first diagnosed, and in due course Kissack was sent to his first mental institution. Further, it was believed that those mental problems might well have been a result of an accident when Kissack fell upon some rocks while out hunting. He had had to endure being trapped for an entire night and most of the following day before help arrived.

Kissack was also known to have a fascination with guns, knew the area well and, furthermore, a man fitting Kissack's description had called at a house in Sulby Glen on the Sunday, asking for some bread. A manhunt was now organized, supervised by the chief constable himself, Colonel Madoc, and it was Colonel Madoc who broke the news of the shooting to Percy's wife and to his son, who was at King William's College.

On the day after the shooting, Tuesday, 14 October, Kissack was seen carrying a shotgun and hiding in a culvert, but by the time the police arrived he had vanished. Officers were drafted into the area, though, and this did lead to his eventual apprehension.

At around 3 p.m., Sergeant Philip Watterson and other police officers, including Constable C.W. Cowin, were searching some ruined houses near Druidale when they found Kissack in one of them, standing near a fireplace, with a dead rabbit close to his feet. Sergeant Watterson surprised his man and ordered him to surrender. Kissack offered no resistance, dropped his gun, and was finally handcuffed. When the gun was checked, it was seen that both barrels were loaded.

The inquest on Percy Brooke opened at Ramsey that same Tuesday before Mr W. Lay, the High Bailiff of Douglas. Only identification evidence was heard, from Robert Lees, Percy's brother-in-law. At 2.30 p.m. the following afternoon, Percy was laid to rest at Lezayre.

It was also on that Wednesday that Kissack made his first court appearance. Only evidence of the arrest was given, during which a brief statement made by Kissack was read out. In this he had said, 'I will tell you what I done. I just levelled the gun to frighten him. If I had any intention of killing, I would have killed the two of them.' The hearing was then adjourned until the following day.

On Thursday, 16 October, Kissack was back in court. William Christian, who had taken his men to surround the cottage, confirmed that he had known Percy Brooke very well – and even that Percy was his landlord. He had been to Lhergyrhenny Cottage before and seen the gun that was now produced in court. Christian confirmed that it had belonged to the dead man and normally hung over a mantelpiece.

After William Kinrade had given his evidence, Dr Kitchen stepped into the witness box. He began by describing the position of the body in the cottage. Percy lay at the foot of the stairs, slightly on his left side with his head just inside the room to the right. There was a large pool of blood and Dr Kitchen estimated that Percy had been dead for two to three hours. A later examination showed a large hole through Percy's clothing and, when this was removed, a wound was seen just over the right shoulder. In Dr Kitchen's opinion, Percy Brooke had been crouching at the time the shot was fired, from somewhere above him.

Having heard all the evidence it was decided to send Kissack for trial on a charge of wilful murder. That trial opened on Friday, 28 November 1930, before Deemster Reginald Douglas Farrant. The prosecution case was led by

Mr Ramsey Bignall Moore who was assisted by Mr George Moore, his son. The case for the defence rested in the hands of Mr John Henry Lockhart Cowin and Mr Howard Lay. Asked how he wished to plead, Kissack replied, 'Not guilty. It was an accident.'

The trial lasted for two days and all the witnesses previously mentioned gave their evidence again. In addition, the defence called George William Corlett, an expert on firearms. He had examined the gun used to kill Percy Brooke, a very rusty, double-barrelled 12-bore shotgun and he agreed that if a man picked up the weapon with his finger on the trigger, it might well have gone off accidentally. Corlett had tested the pull on the weapon and stated that it was 4¼ pounds for the right barrel and 4½ pounds for the left. He had tested other such guns from his shop and found that the usual pressure required to discharge a barrel was up to 7¾ pounds. Further tests had shown that only the right barrel had been fired recently.

Corlett had also visited the scene of the shooting and testified that a man holding the weapon, standing where Kissack must have been, might well catch the stock of the gun on the corner of a partition between the walls. It might well be that Kissack had actually been backing away, with his finger on the trigger, when the gun caught this partition, causing it to go off.

Testimony as to Kissack's sanity was given by no fewer than four doctors: Dr Skene, Dr Pantin, Dr Lionel Woods and Dr Marshall. All agreed that Kissack did not know right from wrong. Evidence was also given that Kissack's mother had suffered from acute melancholia and had died in a mental asylum in 1903.

In his summing up, Deemster Farrant told the jury that there were four possible verdicts open to them. They could find Kissack: not guilty; guilty of murder; guilty of manslaughter; or guilty of murder, but insane. After an adjournment of two and a half hours, the jury returned to court, announced that they could not agree on a verdict, and asked for guidance and advice from the deemster. Eventually, however, after returning to their deliberations, they filed back into court to state that they had found Kissack 'Guilty of murder but insane at the time he committed the offence'.

Whatever the result might have been, Kissack would, at the very least, have been returned to the asylum but now he was sentenced to be detained during His Majesty's Pleasure. In due course he was sent to England and committed to Broadmoor, where he ended his days.

9

Murder at the Golden Egg

On the morning of Wednesday, 15 August 1973, Jean Cowell, a cleaner of Greba Road, turned up as usual for work at the Golden Egg restaurant at 10 Strand Street, Douglas. It was a day Jean would never forget, because when she went into the kitchen at the back she discovered the bound and gagged, dead body of the restaurant manager, 26-year-old Nigel Neal. Jean asked a window cleaner, George Court, who was outside at the time, for assistance and it was he who called the police.

By 8.45 a.m., Dr Joseph H. Ferguson, the police surgeon, was in attendance. He noted that the body was lying face upwards on the floor of a small scullery at the back of the premises. Neal was fully dressed in a shirt, trousers, a butcher's apron and boots. His legs had been tied together at the ankles by a cloth and a piece of rope, while his hands had been secured across the front of his body with a man's necktie, which had then also been tied to the metal leg of a sink unit. There was a gag over Neal's mouth and his face and head were covered in blood. He had been killed by one or more blows to the head with some heavy object, and bloody footprints were found around the body, on the stairs and on the floor of the flat above, where Neal had lived.

Nigel Neal was a married man with two young children. He had trained to be a chef in Coventry and had later worked as joint-manager of a restaurant in Bowness, Cumbria. Soon after this he had moved to Great Harwood where he had

Boots Chemist in Strand Street, Douglas. This was the location of the Golden Egg Restaurant

worked as a night-chef at the local hospital. In May 1973, he had taken the position of manager at the Golden Egg in Douglas. His wife Hilary and their children still lived in Great Harwood, but kept in touch by telephone and Neal would return home whenever he had the chance.

The police now made contact with Hilary Neal and she informed them that she had last seen her husband when he returned home for just one day on 11 July. She was in the habit of telephoning every night when she knew Nigel had finished work. She had last spoken to him on 14 August, and the following day – 15 August – had rung at 12.25 a.m., but there had been no reply. She continued to ring until 2.25 a.m., but without success.

The day after the body had been found, 16 August, the inquest on the dead man opened before the deputy coroner, Mr Kewley, as the coroner, Henry Callow, was on leave. By now Hilary Neal had flown over to the island and she gave formal evidence of identification. Brief details of the cause of death were also given before matters were adjourned pending further enquiries. By now, however, the police were looking for one particular individual.

James Richard Lunney was twenty-one years of age. He had left school in Surrey at the age of sixteen and took various casual jobs in England and Guernsey before coming to the Isle of Man in June 1973. After a brief period of unemployment, Lunney took work as a lorry driver, but this position only lasted for five weeks. One week before Nigel Neal's death, Lunney had started as a grill chef at the Golden Egg and the two men appeared to get on very well. There were, however, other factors, which the police were aware of.

Lunney had a criminal record and had several convictions for burglary and theft. He was wanted by the police for fraud offences and the theft of a coat. It also appeared that, in addition, Lunney had financial problems. He had stayed at several addresses on the island and had moved into 14 Christian Road, Douglas, on 22 July, using the name of Richard Harris. He had soon fallen into arrears with his rent and, on 14 August, the day before Nigel Neal was killed, Lunney had been given notice to leave by his landlady, Ada Elizabeth Taylor. By now it had been determined that the killer had taken around £1,000 from the restaurant. Further, Lunney was nowhere to be found.

Other staff at the Golden Egg had stated that Lunney was not on duty on the day Neal was killed, but he had, nevertheless, been on the premises. Mrs Joan Benson was the night-cashier at the restaurant and she was on duty on the evening of 14 August. Early that evening, Lunney came in and gave her a note which he asked her to pass on to Neal when he was free. At the time, Neal was working in the kitchen, but Joan did indeed hand over the note and saw Neal read it at around 8.30 p.m. Joan could see, from a quick glance, that it said something about an Annette and Joan noticed that Neal looked somewhat annoyed. This mysterious note had been found in Neal's wallet by Sergeant Ralph Kewley. In full it read, 'Nigel, have seen Annette and Chris is back. We'll all be in the lounge bar at the casino if you're interested at 12.30. Richard.'

Joan Benson went on to say that Lunney and Neal were in conversation between 9 p.m. and 10.15 p.m. after which Lunney left the premises. He returned, though, soon after 11 p.m., when he mentioned to her and the other staff that he and Neal intended to go to the casino later. Joan Benson finally left the Golden Egg just before midnight as her husband arrived to give her a lift home. Three other staff left very soon afterwards, sharing the same taxi and, when they left, Neal and Lunney were alone together in the restaurant.

Meanwhile, the weapon used to kill Nigel Neal had been found. On 17 August, Kevin Paul Carey, a griddle-chef, was cleaning up in the restaurant kitchen when he found a blood-stained fire extinguisher underneath the chip fryers. The police were informed and later tests would show that blood on it matched that of the victim. Furthermore, fingerprints on it matched those of Richard Lunney.

Lunney's description was circulated the day after Neal's body had been found. The details stated that in addition to his real name, he was known to use the names of Richard Harris, J. R. Harris and John Sandrey. He had been born on 27 July 1952, in Wimbledon, and was 5 feet 11 inches tall with a fresh complexion. He was well-spoken and had short, light brown hair and blue eyes. When last seen, he was known to be wearing a navy blue coat.

Police investigations showed that Lunney, using the name Sandrey, had checked into the Athol Hotel at 10 p.m. on 14 August. It should be remembered that he had been told to find fresh lodgings by his landlady since he hadn't paid his rent.

A part-time taxi-driver, Geoffrey Walmsley, had come forward to say that at some time between midnight and 12.30 a.m. on 15 August he had been driving his cab along the promenade when he was hailed by a man fitting Lunney's description, who darted out from between parked cars close to the Athol Hotel. The man announced that his wife was seriously ill back in Newcastle, and so he had to get off the island as soon as possible. The man got into Walmsley's cab and was taken up Victoria Street, but suddenly asked to be let out at the top of the street.

By 12.30 a.m., Lunney was back at the Athol as he was seen by staff there who described him as sweating heavily. He volunteered to the manageress that he had received a telegram saying that his wife had been injured in a car crash in Newcastle and said again that he needed to get off the island. After some discussion, Lunney asked if she knew how he might charter a plane and she then made enquiries of a friend who stated that the airport was closed until 7 a.m. Lunney also asked about boats, but was again told that nothing would be moving until the morning. He finally left the bar in the Athol at 12.45 a.m. Just fifteen minutes later, at 1 a.m., he was seen leaving the hotel carrying a black suitcase.

By 1.50 a.m., Lunney was at the Palace Hotel where he booked a room under the name of John Sandrey. He paid with a £5 note and was seen downstairs a number of times. He was finally seen climbing into a taxi in front of the hotel.

That taxi was driven by George Pyatt who had been driving down a deserted promenade at about 6 a.m. on 15 August when he heard a whistle as he passed the Palace Hotel. Looking up, he saw a man signalling to him from a first-floor balcony. The man then came downstairs and asked to be taken to Ronaldsway airport. He carried a small, black, executive-type case. During that journey, Lunney stated that he had made a killing at the casino and had won £300. He also mentioned that he had to get off the island as a relative had been taken ill back in England.

The taxi arrived at the airport at around 6.15 a.m. and Lunney paid the £1.50 fare with two £1 notes. Pyatt could not help but notice that Lunney peeled the notes off a large roll.

The airport was still closed and, even as Lunney was paying his fare, a member of the airport police came out and Pyatt suggested that his passenger should speak to him as he might know where a plane could be hired. That policeman was Ronald Ian Ludgate and he listened to Lunney's story about needing to get to Newcastle urgently. Ludgate contacted a pilot, John Lewis, who was with the Manx Flyers Aero Club, and he agreed to take the man to Blackpool. Lunney then waited with Ludgate for just over an hour during which time the policeman even made his guest a cup of coffee.

John Lewis finally arrived at the airport and asked Lunney to fill out a standard form giving some personal details. Lunney filled it in using the name John Sandrey and gave his home address as 38 Hauteville Street, St Peter Port, Guernsey.

At 7.35 a.m., Lewis and his passenger left Ronaldsway and arrived at Blackpool around 8.05 a.m. It was about this same time that Nigel Neal's body was being discovered by Jean Cowell. Lunney paid £15 for the trip, peeling the cash off a large roll of banknotes. By 8.15 a.m., John Lewis was on his way back to the Isle of Man.

Once all this information had come to the attention of the police, the description of Lunney was then circulated throughout England. It was this that led a taxi-driver to come forward to say that he had picked Lunney up at Blackpool airport and taken him to a garage at Clayton-le-Woods. The garage owner was then spoken to and confirmed that Lunney had purchased a white MGB Roadster for £510 cash. He had also purchased three maps, one of Northern England, and ones for Central and Southern Scotland. The registration number of Lunney's new car – JFV 465F – was then added to the police bulletins.

Further police work led to confirmation that Lunney had stayed briefly at a hotel near Ulverston and had then moved on to Edinburgh, where he was finally apprehended.

At 12.30 a.m. on Friday, 17 August, Constable David Berry saw the white MGB in the car park of the Post House Hotel in Edinburgh. Berry contacted the station and the car was then put under surveillance. At 6.05 a.m., Lunney was seen leaving the hotel, and as soon as he got into the car he was arrested.

He was then taken to the Central Police Station in Parliament Square where he was searched and found to be carrying £331.02 in cash and a bunch of keys – which would later be found to be those to the Golden Egg restaurant.

On the same day that Lunney was arrested, the head of the Manx CID, Haydn Fitzsimmons, and Detective Sergeant Alan Jones travelled to Edinburgh to interview him. Lunney said that he wished to make a written statement after which he was escorted back to Douglas. The following day, Saturday, 18 August, at 7.40 p.m. he was charged with murder – to which he replied: 'Just as I said before, I didn't do it with malice aforethought.' A few days later, on 7 September, he was also charged with robbery with violence.

James Richard Lunney faced his trial at Douglas on 6 December before Deemster R. K. Eason. The case for the prosecution was led by the Attorney General Mr Arthur Luft, who was assisted by Mr Michael Moyle. Lunney was defended by Mr Edwyn Garside and Mr Eric Teare. The proceedings would last for six days, and created a sensation as the first murder trial on the island since 1930.

In addition to the various witnesses already mentioned, the prosecution called Dr Stephen Garratt, the pathologist who had performed the postmortem. He stated that Nigel Neal's death had been caused by several hard blows with a heavy blunt instrument and added that death had not been instantaneous. He gave the time of death as around 1 a.m. on 15 August, plus or minus one hour. That postmortem had been witnessed by Dr Stephen Baker who agreed that death was caused by a cerebral haemorrhage due to a fracture of the skull.

The time came for Lunney to tell his own story. He confirmed the basic details of his arrival on the island and of his commencing work at the Golden Egg about one week before Nigel Neal was killed.

On the day in question, Lunney said he had left the Athol Hotel some time after 10 p.m. on 14 August. He had then walked along Strand Street to a Chinese restaurant, where he had a meal before going on to the Golden Egg to wait for Neal to finish for the night.

By the time he arrived, at close to 11 p.m., the restaurant was already closed and the staff were cleaning up. At one stage, Mr Benson arrived to pick up his wife and they chatted for five minutes or so until she was ready to leave. All the other staff, apart from Neal, left the premises at about 11.45 p.m. He and Neal then chatted, and at one stage had a drink together in the restaurant before Neal went back into the kitchen to finish tidying up.

They started talking about women and Lunney claimed that Neal had wanted an introduction to a friend of his named Annette. An argument started during which Lunney reminded Neal that he was a married man. At this, Neal had taken a wild swing at him. A fight started and the two men fell to the floor.

Neal pulled away, stood up, and took a pan from a rack above the sink and tried to hit Lunney with it. It had only been at that point that Lunney had grabbed a fire extinguisher and hit Neal two or three times on the head. As Neal fell to the floor, Lunney saw that his own shirt front was covered in blood so he removed it, went upstairs to the flat above the premises, washed the blood off his hands and arms, and then put on a sweatshirt he had found. He then went back downstairs and left through the front door, locking it behind him with the keys – which he had found on one of the work surfaces.

After ten or fifteen minutes, Lunney had gone back to the restaurant and let himself in. Looking around now, he found a brown paper bag with money in it, next to the cash desk. He also found the keys to the safe, which was upstairs. Opening it, he found a pile of banknotes, which he also took, but at that point he heard a noise from downstairs.

Going to investigate he found Neal, groaning on the floor. He was trying to get up but was unable to do so. Believing that the injured man would be fine until the following morning, he then tied him up and gagged him but made sure that he was able to breathe. As Lunney had said when interviewed, 'He looked bloody, but he didn't look like he was going to die.' Finally, leaving the restaurant for the last time, Lunney confirmed that he had gone to the Palace Hotel and taken a room there before deciding to flee to the mainland.

On the sixth day of the trial the jury retired to consider their verdict. After a deliberation of one hour, they returned to announce that they had found Lunney guilty on two counts: murder and robbery with violence. Lunney was then sentenced to death by hanging.

It was never expected that the sentence would be carried out and it came as no surprise when the Home Secretary of the day, Robert Carr, commuted the sentence to one of life imprisonment. The first case of murder on the island in forty-three years was over.

10

The Man from Onchan

Michael John Howard was a successful businessman and the managing director of Howard Amusements Limited. He lived in Douglas and each night parked his car in a garage in Market Street, at the back of the Strand Cinema.

It was 10.15 p.m. on Wednesday, 31 May 1978, Michael Howard and his wife pulled into Market Street to put the car away for the night. To his surprise, Mr Howard noticed that the folding doors to the garage were slightly open. As he waited in the driver's seat, his wife got out to open the doors fully, but what she found behind those doors would horrify her.

The body of a young girl lay behind one door. There was a good deal of blood on her head and face, her jeans had been pulled down and her panties torn off and thrown on to her chest. The Howards immediately contacted the police.

It was a simple matter to identify the poor girl. Her white T-shirt had been pushed high on to her chest, but when it was examined it was found to have a slogan: 'I like it when I can get it'. The shirt also bore a name: Janice. It wasn't long before 'Janice' had been formally identified as a young woman missing from a nearby guest house – Janice McCallum.

Janice McCallum was an 18-year-old from Largs in Scotland. She lived with a girlfriend, Anne Cuthbertson, and the two girls had come to the island for a holiday on Sunday, 28 May. They had originally booked into the Ravenswood Hotel in Clifton Terrace, but their money started to run out so they moved on 31 May to the guest house at 1 Castle Mona Avenue.

Speaking to Anne Cuthbertson, police officers discovered that she and Janice had spent some time that evening at the Broadway Bar in the Central Hotel. It was while they were in the bar that Janice said she was going to ask their landlady, Mrs Kelly, if she could take her puppy, Biggles, for a walk. Mrs Kelly apparently agreed, because when Janice returned to the bar some minutes later she had the dog with her. By the time Janice left for her walk, it was close to 10 p.m.

Anne stayed in the bar with another resident of the guest house, John Bow, before they both went back to Castle Mona Avenue at around 10.45 p.m. To Anne's surprise, Janice hadn't yet returned so she and John went out to look for her. They did not know that Janice's body had already been found in the garage in Market Street.

There was, however, no sign of the missing dog, Biggles. Joyce Prescott worked at a cinema in Strand Street and it had been around 10.30 p.m. on 31 May when she left the cinema and walked down Market Street. She found the puppy running around with a lead still attached, so she caught it and looked around for the owner. When she couldn't find anyone, Joyce let the dog go, concluding that it would probably find its own way home. In fact, a man who ran his own taxi company found the puppy minutes later, took it home, and then took it to the police station the following morning. The dog was, of course, subsequently shown to be Biggles.

The police made every effort to find the killer of Janice McCullum. A scientific team from the North West Forensic Science Laboratory at Chorley and a number of officers from Lancashire were flown in to assist their Manx colleagues, the inquiry being led by Chief Superintendent Wilf Brooks. An incident room was set up close to the murder scene. Posters and flyers asking for information were printed and distributed, and officers searched the luggage of people leaving the island in case the bags contained bloodstained clothing.

On Friday, 2 June, a female volunteer, wearing clothing identical to the items Janice had been wearing, retraced the route she had taken on the night she died. This volunteer even led the puppy, Biggles, on that walk and valuable witnesses came forward as a result.

It was also on 2 June that the inquest on Janice McCallum opened in Douglas before the deputy coroner, Mr Weldon Williams.

The first witness was Janice's mother who had flown over from Scotland to identify her daughter's body. She confirmed that Janice had lived with her until September 1977 when she had left home and started living with Anne Cuthbertson. Her daughter had worked as a shop-assistant and the last time she had spoken to Janice was on the evening of Tuesday, 30 May, when they had chatted on the telephone.

Dr Roger Harry Ritson, the police surgeon, had been called to the garage on the night of 31 May and arrived there at 10.45 p.m. He estimated that Janice had been dead for anything up to two hours, though the testimony of other witnesses would later narrow down the time of the attack to some time between 10 p.m. and 10.15 p.m.

Listing the injuries, Dr Ritson reported a 2-centimetre split in the left corner of Janice's mouth. There were two areas of clotted blood on her face – one over the right eyebrow and one on the left side. Janice's jeans had been pulled down to around her ankles and this had been done with some force as they had also been ripped at the seams. Her panties had been torn into two pieces and lay on her upper chest.

Dr Brian Beeson was a Home Office pathologist and he had performed the postmortem at 2 p.m. on 1 June. He reported a number of bruises and grazes on Janice's body. She had also sustained a broken nose and other facial bone fractures. In his opinion, the injuries would have required a minimum of four blows. In addition to these injuries, there were marks on Janice's neck, which indicated pressure, and the cause of death was asphyxia caused by that pressure and blood inhalation.

John Bow, who had been in the bar at the Central Hotel with

Anne Cuthbertson, confirmed that Janice had come in with their landlady's puppy and had left again at around 10 p.m.

After Joyce Prescott reported her finding of the dog in Market Street at about 10.30 p.m., a number of witnesses were called who had seen a woman fitting Janice's description after she had left the Central Hotel bar.

Christine Carphily had been in the Wimpy Bar in Strand Street with her boyfriend and they left that establishment together at 10 p.m. Christine was sure of the time as she wanted to catch the last bus to her home in Willaston and that left at 10.25 p.m.

Christine said that as she and her boyfriend strolled towards Granville Street they saw Janice coming towards them from the opposite direction. They remembered her distinctive T-shirt with its slogan and that she had a small dog on a lead. At the time, Janice was alone.

Vivian Woods left the Strand Cinema and briefly visited a nearby public house called the Dog's Home before walking back up along Strand Street. She saw a young couple walking by the cinema. At first she took little notice of them, but then the girl almost fell over the lead of the dog she was walking. The man who was with her then put his arm around her to steady her. They were certainly together for they then walked off holding hands. The general description of the young woman – 5 feet 3 inches tall, brown hair, wearing a white top and blue jeans, and the fact that she had a small dog – did fit Janice, but Vivian only ever saw them properly from behind so couldn't be 100 per cent sure it was Janice. As for the man, he was taller by a good 6 inches, of medium build, and was wearing a white shirt and dark trousers. Vivian estimated his age as early twenties. The inquest was adjourned until the following week, but there would be a major development in the meantime.

On Sunday, 4 June, Sergeant John Teare was called to a house in Douglas. A woman had telephoned the police and informed them that she had found her husband dead in bed.

The sergeant drove to a house in Onchan, and soon determined that the dead man fitted the general description of the man who had been seen with Janice McCallum on the night she died. This and other findings led to a number of items being taken from the house – including a pair of trainers that had been found underneath a pile of clothing in the hallway.

When the inquest was resumed, Philip Charles Rydeard, a Home Office forensic scientist, stated that he had photographed and measured a number of footprints left in the dust on the garage floor where Janice's body had been found. The prints had been made by a pair or trainers, and Mr Rydeard had compared his photos to the tread and wear patterns on the trainers taken from the house at Onchan. His conclusion was that it was highly unlikely that the prints in the garage could have been made by any other footwear – it was a *possibility*, but a very remote one. Other witnesses were now called who had had some dealings with the man from Onchan who had been found dead in his bed.

Robert John Kelso had known the man for some five years. On 31 May, Kelso had been in the bar at the Regent Hotel, with a friend, Michael Cowin, at around 5 p.m. At 6.30 p.m., the man from Onchan came in and joined them. Some women came into the bar and the man went off with one of them, Valerie Agnew. He returned alone, before 8.30 p.m., and Kelso bought him a drink as he pointed out that he had no money.

The three men sat together drinking, but then a young woman came in. She was wearing a white T-shirt, with a slogan on the chest, and had a small dog with her. It was then that the man from Onchan announced, in the crudest of terms, that he was going to have sex with her. He went over to talk to her and returned a few minutes later to finish his glass of beer before leaving the bar, with the young woman.

Michael Cowin confirmed this testimony, but added that when the man had left he appeared to be quite drunk.

Valerie Agnew said she had seen the three men in the bar together. She had known the man from Onchan for about three months and had left the bar with him at about 6.30 p.m. They went to the Dog's Home public house and had a drink together. When they left, she went on to the Athol while he said he was going back to the Regent.

John Houghton had been out with his girlfriend on the night of 31 May and they saw the man, whom he knew quite well, in Strand Street at some time around 9.45 p.m. Later, John and his girlfriend went to look at the new multi-storey car park in Chester Street and decided to go to the top to take in the view. While they were up there, Houghton saw the man again. He was walking directly beneath them, from the direction of Strand Street towards Church Road. It was then about 10.20 p.m.

The next witness was Detective Chief Inspector Moore who had measured the length of two possible routes between the garage where Janice's body was discovered, to the house at Onchan. One distance, the shorter one, was 2.4 miles while the other was 2.7 miles. This was of significance because the evidence of the next witness was to contradict the testimony of Kelso, Cowin, Houghton and Valerie Agnew.

The dead man's wife claimed that her husband had arrived home at 10 p.m. on 31 May. She had been in bed at the time and he brought her up a cup of coffee. She was sure of the time because the news was just starting on the television. He then got undressed and climbed into bed beside her.

The woman confirmed that her husband had been depressed of late. He was unemployed and they had financial concerns. In fact, his state of mind had deteriorated so much that some weeks before she had insisted that he visit his doctor. He seemed to get better after this, possibly because of the medication he was now taking.

The medical evidence showed that the man had died from an overdose of Tuinal, a sedative barbiturate. No suicide note had been found.

The proceedings of this dual investigation lasted a full week and then, after a three-hour deliberation, the jury gave their verdict that the man from Onchan had taken his own life, and that he was also the man responsible for the murder of Janice McCallum. The team of detectives and forensic scientists returned to England and the inquiry closed down.

The man from Onchan was not named at the time of the investigation into Janice McCallum's death. It can now be revealed that he was actually a man named Michael Kelly.

11

Uncle Jack

Gary Kenneth Tansell was puzzled. It was most unusual for John Gale Bridson to be away from his home at 114 Malew Street, Castletown, for such a long time.

Gary Tansell had last seen Bridson on Tuesday, 25 September 1979. He next called at the house on Sunday, 30 September, with a lady friend, but there was no reply to his knocking. The curtains were drawn but as there was a bottle of milk on the front doorstep, Gary assumed that Bridson had just gone to the shops. However, when he called back that afternoon, there was still no reply, but now there were two pints of milk on the doorstep. Going to a nearby telephone box, Gary rang the house but got the engaged tone. Surely this required further investigation.

Going back to number 114, Gary Tansell went around to the back of the house. Again there were no signs of life but the door, though closed, was unlocked. Tentatively, Gary stepped into the house.

The sound of some music came from upstairs. Going up to investigate, Gary found that the music was coming from Bridson's bedroom, so Gary knocked gently on the door. From within came the sound of Bridson's dogs whimpering and some other sound – a muffled noise that seemed like a sleepy voice far away. Deciding that Mr Bridson was probably entertaining someone, or possibly sleeping off the effects of a night's drinking, Gary Tansell thought it better to leave.

By Tuesday, 2 October, the neighbours too were growing somewhat concerned. Rosemary Dawson, who lived at 100

Malew Street, had not seen John Bridson since Friday, 28 September. Two days later, on the Sunday, she noticed that there were now two pints of milk on the doorstep. The final straw came on Tuesday, 2 October, when she noticed that the curtains were still drawn upstairs at 11.30 a.m. John Bridson was an early riser, and she thought that if he were still in bed at this late hour, then perhaps he had been taken ill. Rosemary checked with some of the other neighbours to see if anyone had seen John Bridson and, when they all said no, she took her concerns to the police.

Constable Ian Young arrived at the house at around 12.30 p.m. on Tuesday, 2 October, in the company of Constable Paul John Davenport. They too found the back door unlocked and went inside to investigate.

Dogs could be heard barking furiously upstairs and, as the two officers drew closer to the bedroom door, they heard deep growling from within. Concerned that the dogs might be

114 Malew Street, the home of John Gale Bridson in 1979

vicious, Constable Young opened the bedroom door just a fraction. Even with that restricted view, he could see a man's leg lying on the floor near the bed and signs that the man had been tied up with some plastic wire. Going downstairs to telephone for help, Young saw that the instrument had been torn from the wall. He radioed the police station, told his superiors what he had found, and requested assistance to deal with the dogs.

Robert Henry Teare, an RSPCA inspector, arrived at the house soon afterwards and carefully removed the dogs from the bedroom. Now, for the first time, Constable Young could enter the room and make a careful examination of the scene.

The body of a man lay face down on the floor at the side of the bed. His feet had been tied together, and his hands were also tied behind his back. There were pillows over his head and the body had also been tied to the bed.

Nothing was disturbed until Dr John Edward Brewis arrived to make his examination. The pillows were now removed and Dr Brewis saw that most of the man's face had been covered with white shiny tape. In fact, he was covered from below the nose to underneath the chin. From below this tape, the end of a necktie protruded.

The body was duly identified as that of John Gale Bridson, known widely as Jack. Bridson had been in the RAF and, after leaving the forces, had served as holiday relief postman. He was also a football referee. He had lived alone with his two dogs and, it seemed, was rather fond of young men.

Investigations soon showed that Bridson had a particular male friend – 27-year-old Graham Ralph Frankland, who called him Uncle Jack. Further, Frankland had actually been seen in Bridson's house very recently.

Sandra May Dickson, who before her marriage had actually been engaged to Frankland, was on the way to her sister's house in Castletown at 8.45 p.m. on Friday, 28 September, and passed down Malew Street. She particularly noted number 114 because she knew that he had lived there with his 'Uncle Jack' when they were engaged some seven years before. She saw that all the lights in the house were on and, as she passed number 114, she saw Frankland standing by the window in the front room.

Frankland had also been seen, driving Bridson's car, on the Saturday. Mona Elizabeth Holmes also lived in Malew Street, so knew Bridson's car well. She had seen it pass her on the bridge in Castletown at around 6.50 p.m. on Saturday, 29 September, and recognized Frankland as the driver. He was alone at the time.

In fact, the police did not have to look very far to find Graham Frankland. Later, on 2 October, the day John Bridson's body was discovered, he was seen heading back towards Malew Street and was taken in for questioning. It wasn't very long before Frankland, an unemployed general worker of 14 Peel Road, Douglas, was admitting to tying up John Bridson. As a result, he was arrested by Detective Sergeant Dudley Butt, and formally charged with murder at 3.00 a.m. on Wednesday, 3 October. He was also charged with the theft, with violence, of the sum of £70.

Various remands followed and, in due course, Frankland's committal proceedings began at Castle Rushen, Castletown, on Monday, 10 December. After the evidence had been heard, Frankland was sent for trial. That trial opened before Deemster Arthur Luft on Monday, 14 April 1980. The case for the prosecution was led by Mr Michael Moyle while Frankland was defended by Mr Eric Teare.

Dr Brian Beeson, the Home Office pathologist, stated that he had found several ligature marks on the body, which lay on the floor but remained tied to the bed. Death had been due to respiratory failure as a consequence of being tied up. However, Dr Beeson was able to add that he had detected signs of a lung condition and heart disease and these would certainly have been contributory factors. Finally, in Dr Beeson's opinion, death might have occurred two days prior to the discovery of the body – that is, on or about 30 September.

Arthur Franklin Crow was a milkman who delivered to

John Bridson. He told the court that Mr Bridson took milk on Sundays, Tuesdays, Thursdays and Saturdays and it was his routine to collect the money due each Saturday.

On Saturday, 29 September, Crow had left one pint of milk on Bridson's doorstep. There was, however, no answer to his knocking when he tried to collect the money he was owed. On the Sunday, he saw that the previous day's milk was still there. This had happened before so he thought nothing of it and left another pint. On the Tuesday, however, the two bottles were still there and he assumed that Mr Bridson had gone on holiday and forgotten to cancel his milk. Crow then took away the two old bottles and replaced them with a new one. This testimony implied two things. First, that Bridson had been tied up by Saturday, 29 September, and, since the time of death was given at around 30 September, he had spent two days or more tied to his bed before he died.

Detective Constable Ian Bradshaw had made a search of the premises at Malew Street after Bridson's body had been removed. He had found a number of pornographic books, of a homosexual nature, in a bedside cabinet, thus reinforcing what was known about Bridson's sexual proclivities.

Mr Michael Firth, a forensic scientist from the Home Office Forensic Science Laboratory at Chorley, had flown over to the island to examine the scene in the bedroom. He reported that a two-core electric cable had been looped around the upper part of Bridson's body and around the bed itself. It was tied around the upper legs of the bed and then, in a double loop, around both ankles. In Mr Firth's opinion, John Bridson had originally been placed upon the bed, but in his struggle to escape the cable had fallen off on to the floor.

Graham Frankland had readily admitted tying Bridson to his bed, but said that his intention had not been to kill. He began by saying that he had lived with 'Uncle Jack' when he was just fourteen years old, when he had first come to the Isle of Man. A few days before Friday, 28 September, he had gone to see Bridson at his house and told him that he intended marrying his girlfriend, Monica Farrell. An argument had then started between them and at one stage Bridson had said that he would tell Monica that Frankland was 'queer'.

On the Friday, Frankland had been drinking and decided that he simply couldn't let this happen. He went back to Bridson's house, hoping to talk him out of saying anything to Monica. When it became clear that Bridson would not be moved on this, Frankland attacked him, subdued him, and tied him to his bed. He knew that Monica was due to leave the island early the following week and his intention was to keep him in his house until after she left. After that, he would free Bridson and try to reason with him again.

The next time Frankland had gone to Malew Street was on the Sunday, but he didn't go in as there were a lot of people about. He was on his way to free Bridson on 2 October when he was arrested by the police. Finally, Frankland said he knew that Bridson was a homosexual, but denied that there had ever been any form a sexual relationship between them, even when he had lived with Bridson.

At least part of this testimony was confirmed by Monica Farrell herself. She told the court that she was twenty-one and lived near Dublin. She had come to work on the island on 3 June 1979, and had taken a job at the Sefton Hotel in Douglas. That was where she had first met Frankland who soon introduced her to his 'Uncle Jack'.

On the evening of Friday, 28 September to Saturday, 29 September, she was with Frankland and two friends of theirs – Brian and Cathy Corrie – in the Tramshunters Bar, Douglas. It was around 9.45 p.m. and Frankland told them that he had been to see his uncle who had given him permission to use his car. That night, Frankland spent money freely and she asked him where he had got it from as she knew he was unemployed. He said that his uncle had given it to him and, in return, he was to do some painting for him.

That Saturday, she and Frankland drove around the island in his uncle's car. At one stage she asked if they might go to see

Jack, but Frankland explained that he had gone away for the weekend. He also claimed that his uncle intended giving him the car for his birthday.

The verdict, when it came, was that Frankland was guilty on both charges: murder and theft with violence. He was then sentenced to death and immediately announced his intention to appeal.

That appeal was heard on Tuesday, 1 July, before the judge of appeal, Iain Glidewell, and the acting deemster, Douglas Brown. Mr Kenneth Quilleash now appeared for Frankland.

The defence claimed that there had been misdirection by Deemster Luft with regard to his definition of malice afore-thought and robbery with violence. Mr Quilleash admitted that if his client were indeed guilty of robbery with violence then, in law, he must also be guilty of murder. However, Frankland had claimed that the £70 he had admitted taking from Bridson's wallet was money that Bridson had freely given. There was no evidence to support a claim of robbery with violence.

In part, Frankland was successful. His appeal on the robbery charge was granted. The court explained that, at the original trial, the jury had returned to court after deliberating for two hours, asking for guidance on the charge of robbery with violence. Deemster Luft had, in his advice, made no reference to Frankland's claim that he had rights to that money and had taken it in good faith. This did amount to misdirection and that charge would be dismissed. There was, however, no misdirection on the murder charge and that conviction was upheld.

The death sentence was, as expected, commuted to one of life imprisonment by the Home Secretary of the day, William Whitelaw, but the story of Graham Ralph Frankland did not end there.

In early March 1987, Frankland was granted a second appeal before five judges sitting in the Privy Council in London. Here it was held that there had been misdirection of the jury at the original trial on the issue of an intention to kill or to cause serious bodily harm.

The murder conviction was quashed and a manslaughter verdict substituted. On that charge, Frankland was sentenced to serve a total of nine years in prison.

12

Bob the Hat

At around 8 p.m. on Tuesday, 8 July 1980, the plane from London landed at Ronaldsway airport. One of the passengers on that flight was 38-year-old David Kenneth Cooke.

One of the first things David Cooke tried to do was hire a car. He walked over to the Athol Garage booth where he spoke to Debbie Jones. Unfortunately, she was unable to assist him as Cooke had not brought his driving licence with him. She would later say that, as he left, Cooke was looking rather annoyed.

Cooke's mood was probably made all the worse when he then found that there were no taxis free to take him to his destination. Fortunately for Cooke, Linda Cregeen, an information officer at the airport, was kind enough to offer Cooke a lift in her car. So it was that, finally, David Cooke arrived at Brook Cottage in Ballabeg. At about the same time that Cooke was entering the cottage, Robert Ward, a business associate of Cooke's, was leaving the Creek Inn at Peel.

Approximately one hour later, at around 9 p.m., Cooke was seen outside Brook Cottage by Ian Crane, a builder from Ballasalla. Cooke whistled to Crane to attract his attention and then asked him if he had seen Bob Ward. When Crane replied that he hadn't, Cooke again looked somewhat annoyed.

Immediately after this, Patrick Bailey, a taxi-driver from Port Erin, received a call to go to Brook Cottage, but first he was to detour to the Colby Glen Hotel to pick up Robert Ward. Bailey did as he was asked but, upon arriving at the hotel, found that Ward wasn't there. He then proceeded to Ballabeg and informed Cooke that he had been unable to find his first fare. Cooke replied that it didn't matter, adding that he had now sacked Ward, as he had failed to do a job for him. Cooke got into Bailey's taxi and was then taken to Peel where he was dropped off at the breakwater. He asked Bailey to wait for him while he briefly boarded a boat, the *Boy Tad*. Very soon afterwards, Cooke asked Bailey to take him to the Creek Inn, then back to the boat and then, finally, back to the Creek Inn. During these journeys, Cooke talked occasionally about Ward, and at one stage described him as a drunken swine.

It was 9.45 p.m. when Cooke made his second visit to the Creek Inn. He asked the landlord, Robert McAleer, if he had seen Bob the Hat, the nickname by which Robert Ward was widely known. McAleer said he had been in earlier and, when he arrived, had ordered two bottles of brandy which he had taken away with him, saying that Cooke would pay for them

The Creek Inn at Peel, visited by both David Cooke and Robert Ward in 1980

when he came in. This did not improve Cooke's mood, but he did pay for the brandy before asking one of the locals – David Taylor, who lived in Station Road, Peel – if he would come back to the breakwater with him and start up the engine of Cooke's boat, the *Boy Tad*.

The two men went back to the boat and Taylor tried in vain to start the engine, informing Cooke that it was no use as the batteries were flat. At this, Cooke said that he would pay him £100 if he could get it going Taylor found some jump leads, but still the engine would not kick into life – whereupon Cooke increased his offer to £150. But it was all to no avail. The engine was well and truly dead.

Even as the attempts to start the boat engine were being made, Robert Ward had returned to the Creek Inn but he didn't stay very long. Robert McAleer would later say that, at this time, Ward was very drunk indeed. Meanwhile, Cooke had given up trying to get the boat's engine started and returned to the cottage. As for Ward, he returned to the Creek Inn at around 10.20 p.m., staying there until close to midnight. It was then that Terrance Shepherd, another taxi-driver, was asked to take Ward to Brook Cottage and to get him there as fast as possible. In fact, a number of times Ward asked Shepherd to '… go faster'. It was, however, well past midnight when Ward was dropped off at the cottage.

John Qualtrough was busily delivering milk as usual on the morning of Wednesday, 9 July 1980 when, at 8 a.m. he came to Brook Cottage. All thoughts of the milk round were soon forgotten because there, in the doorway of the cottage, lay the body of a man. Qualtrough wasted no time in calling the police.

Investigations showed that the dead man was Robert Ward. Inside the house the police had found a second man, David Cooke, asleep on a settee. They had also found a single-barrelled pump action 12-bore shotgun on a rug in the living room. Cooke was then taken into custody for questioning concerning the shooting of Robert Ward.

The story that Cooke told was a most curious one. He explained that he had rung Ward, from England, on 8 July, told him that he would be arriving on the island that evening, and asked him to get his boat, the *Boy Tad*, ready for sea. He had also asked Ward to have a pistol ready for him on the boat, and to have a car waiting for him at the airport.

Cooke then detailed his flight to Ronaldsway, his failed attempt to hire a car, and of finally obtaining a lift from Linda Cregeen. Arriving at Brook Cottage, he had to climb in through an open window in the bathroom as he didn't have any keys with him.

Continuing his narrative, Cooke told officers of his trip to Peel and finding that Ward was not in the Creek Inn and of his subsequent attempts to get someone else to start his boat's engine. Finally, he had given up and returned to the cottage where he again gained entry by climbing in through the bathroom window.

As he entered, Cooke claimed that he heard a noise of some kind, apparently coming from the lounge. He called out, 'Is that you, Bob?', but there was no reply. Going into the lounge he found, to his horror, that a gun was being rammed against the side of his head and a second man then appeared in front of him. This man asked Cooke if he owned the *Boy Tad* and he confirmed that he did. The man standing in front of Cooke then asked his companion, 'Shall we be taking him as well?', but the first man had replied, 'No, it's too dangerous.'

After some minutes of discussion, Cooke was given a glass of brandy and told to knock it back. This was, presumably, some form of Dutch courage for Cooke was now informed that when Ward arrived at the cottage, he would have to shoot him. If he refused, then Cooke's wife, Carol, would be killed. In fact, Cooke never did have to carry out this grim task as he claimed that he had passed out soon afterwards, implying that there might well have been some drug in the brandy he had been forced to drink. He did wake up at one stage and saw a body lying on the floor, but passed out again.

The next thing he knew, he said, was that he was being woken up by the police.

Later, this story was elaborated on somewhat when Cooke admitted that he had severe financial problems and had actually intended to commit suicide. His plan had been to sail out from Peel and throw himself into the sea, but once he had arrived on the island he changed his mind and he was just making himself something to eat when he heard the noise in the lounge. Cooke also confirmed that the gun found at the scene belonged to him and was kept in Brook Cottage. In due course, however, once further investigations had been made, David Kenneth Cooke was formally charged with the murder of Robert Ward.

Cooke's trial opened on Monday, 19 January 1981, and would last until Tuesday, 3 February. The case for the prosecution was outlined by Mr Michael Moyle, while Cooke was defended by Mr Peter Wood who was assisted by Mr John Crellin.

One of the early witnesses was Constable Giles Butterworth who had produced a plan of the area, showing that Ward's body had been found at the entrance to the cottage. The corpse was just inside the doorway, but his feet lay in the porch and it appeared that he had been dragged to that spot. Asked if he had considered that the body had been moved so that it would be discovered, Constable Butterworth said that he was unable to comment.

Rosemary Hawke said that at the time of Ward's death she was employed by Orchid Silks Limited, which operated from premises in Bucks Road. The defendant, David Cooke, was one of the company directors. In July she had been telephoned by Cooke who asked her to make two flight reservations for him. The first was from London to Ronaldsway on 8 July, and the second was a return flight for the following day. She also testified that at one stage Ward had been employed by Orchid Silks, adding that he always appeared to be 'hard up' and that he drank quite heavily.

Geoffrey Albert Brew lived at 5 Albany Close, Peel, and said that he had known Cooke since the summer of 1977 and they had been business partners for a time. He had also known the dead man since 1979 when he had done some work on Cooke's boat, the *Boy Tad*.

Brew stated that at around 1.30 p.m. on 8 July 1980 he had met Ward, by arrangement, in the Colby Glen Hotel. From there they had gone to Peel in Brew's car and he had dropped Ward on the quayside so that he could do some more work on the boat. The two men met again at 5.30 p.m. when Brew picked him up at the quayside and took him to Brook Cottage. By this time, Ward was quite drunk, but while the two men were at the cottage he still managed to consume another half-bottle of whisky. From there, Brew took Ward to Douglas so that he could pick something up from his flat and then took him back to Peel – by which time it was around 8 p.m.

There then followed some legal argument over an approach made to Brew by Cooke's defence before the trial. Mr Moyle said this was an improper approach as it had been made without his knowledge, but it was ruled that no witness was the property of either party so the approach had been quite legal.

The purpose of this approach had been to obtain information about men who might well have been seeking to do some harm to Robert Ward. Brew was now able to testify that one night in May 1979 he had been taking some supplies to Cooke's boat when he noticed that there was a light burning on the vessel. As he got out of his car, two men approached from the boat and asked if he knew Fleetwood Bob, another name by which Ward was known. Brew replied that he did, whereupon he was told to inform Ward that the boys from Portovgie were after him. Brew had then gone to Ward's flat and told him of this encounter. Ward looked very frightened and seemed to be in fear of his life, and added that he had a gun on the premises to protect himself – though he would not say why he might need that protection.

Over the next few weeks, Ward did mention that he had had some trouble from the time he was in Ireland. Part of the reason for these men looking for him might well be because he had been involved with another man's wife, and part might be because he had been in the British armed forces.

One other piece of information from Brew was that while he and Ward were at Brook Cottage, Ward had telephoned his brother, told him to get a pen and to write down the single word 'Highmoor', adding that if anything happened to him his brother would know why. It was pointed out that Cooke had once owned a restaurant named Highmoor.

Further information on the possibility of men looking to cause harm to Ward was given by Thomas William Craine, a joiner from Hillside Avenue in Douglas. He had met Ward, on 8 July, in the Raglan Hotel at around 8.45 p.m. and said that he appeared to be in a very good mood. Previously Ward had mentioned that he had changed his name after some trouble in Ireland, and that once he had stayed at a friend's house in Peel, saying that some Irish lads were after him.

Dr John Moore, of the Home Office Forensic Science Laboratory at Chorley, said that he had gone to Brook Cottage on 9 July 1980. Ward was lying on his back in the doorway of the cottage and had been shot twice: once in the chest and once in the abdomen. There were signs that the body had been dragged from one side of the living room to the doorway as there were large smears of blood on the carpet. Blood spattering was consistent with Ward being shot at least once while he was lying on the floor, close to the television set in the living room. As for Ward's blood being found on the accused, Dr Moore had found a small amount on the heel of Cooke's left sock and, under cross examination, he agreed that this could have landed on Cooke's clothing while he was sleeping.

John Burns, a firearms expert from the Home Office Forensic Science Laboratory in Nottingham, had examined a pump action shotgun which was capable of firing five cartridges without reloading. He estimated that Ward had been shot from a range of four to five feet.

Dr Herbert Barnford had taken blood samples from both Ward and Cooke and reported that Cooke had 178 milligrams of alcohol per 100 millilitres of blood. The figure for Ward was 322 milligrams.

A brandy glass had been found at the scene and this was tested by Michael John Lewis of the Chorley laboratory. It should be remembered that Cooke's statement had implied that he had been rendered unconscious after drinking this brandy, but Lewis reported that there was no evidence of any drug in the glass.

Dr Brian Beeson had performed the postmortem on Ward. He confirmed that there were two wounds and stated that either would have proved fatal.

The defence called 'Mrs X', a woman whose name was only revealed to the deemster and the jury, on a piece of paper. She stated that she had known Robert Ward for six years. They had first met in England, but when she returned to the Isle of Man four years previously they met up again and he told her that he had just come over from Ireland. He seemed to be a different man to her – frightened and filled with bitterness and hatred.

One evening, three years or so before, they had been in the Marine Hotel in Peel when three men came into the bar. Immediately Ward had run out of the rear door and seemed to be in genuine fear for his life. Having said that, Mrs X confirmed that Ward was a 'romancer' who invented stories about himself. He had, for instance, told her that when he was in the army he was a member of the SAS. In fact, Ward had been in the Ordnance Corp.

The time came for Cooke to give his own testimony. He confirmed that initially he had admitted shooting Ward but then, in a statement made on 21 July, he had told the story about the two men waiting in the cottage who were looking for Ward. He explained his earlier admission by saying that he had been afraid that if he told the truth, the two men would carry out their threat to murder his wife. As for the reason for his intention to commit suicide, Cooke told the court that he had been a successful businessman until July 1977 when a restaurant he owned, the Georgians at Stilton, had burned down. The insurance company refused to pay out and later he was charged with several counts, including arson. His trial for these offences was nearing completion in England when he came to the Isle of Man, intending to do away with himself.

On 3 February, the jury retired to consider their verdict. After two and a half hours they returned to announce that they had found Cooke not guilty of murder, but guilty of manslaughter. There followed a delay of some days while various pleas in mitigation were made but then, on Thursday, 12 February 1981, David Kenneth Cooke was sentenced to six years' imprisonment.

13

The Gate Keeper

Michael Camp and Michael John Pate were friends and often went out together even though, at 21, Pate was Camp's senior by close on four years.

Pate would sometimes call at Camp's house in Barrule Drive, Onchan, and did so on the evening of 5/6 April 1981. Camp's father, Edwin Archer Camp, saw Pate and was shocked to hear him say that he had been back to his grandfather's house in Castletown, where he was living, and found him dead on the floor. Edwin Camp told Pate that he should take this information to the police and advised him to visit the police station in Douglas, but Pate said he was going back to Castletown and would report the matter there.

Pate did indeed return to Castletown and it was there, at 1.30 a.m. on 6 April, that he spoke to Constable Brian Rudd and told him that he thought his grandfather, the old gate-house-keeper, was dead.

The man Pate had been referring to was Richard Ormrod Lindesay who had been born in Durban in South Africa on 15 May 1901. As a young infant, Richard and his family had moved to England, where he had grown up. During the Second World War, Richard had first served as an ambulance man and later joined the RAF. He had come to live on the Isle of Man some time around 1957 and had never married.

At 4 a.m. on 6 April, Dr Robert Frederick Jackson attended the Ballawoods Gatehouse at Ballasalla where he viewed the body of Richard Lindesey. The man lay spreadeagled on the kitchen floor and, in Dr Jackson's opinion, had been dead for some twenty-four hours. There were two small cuts on the back of Lindesey's head, but these did not appear to be recent. In fact, there were no obvious signs of injury on the body so the doctor said he was unable to give a cause of death until the postmortem had been performed.

The next day, 7 April, Dr Jackson made a more thorough examination of the body. He found bruises on the neck and others on the chest and deduced that these latter marks might just possibly be bites.

In the meantime, Michael Pate was being interviewed by the police. In his first statement, given to Constable Donald Moyer, Pate said that he had spent the weekend in Douglas, had arrived home at the gatehouse at 1.30 a.m. on Monday, 6 April, and found Lindesey lying dead in the kitchen. Not sure what to do, he had gone to a friend's house – that of Michael Camp – and, acting on advice received there, had reported the matter to the police in Castletown.

Constable Moyer did not accept this version of events and continued to question Pate. In due course Pate made a second statement in which he admitted being present when Lindesey had met his death. According to Pate, Lindesey had made a sexual advance by asking Pate to take his trousers down. Pate had sought to protect himself and hit out at Lindesey, and pushed him. The push had caused the old man to fall and become unconscious, whereupon Pate had then struck him about ten times in the stomach in, apparently, an attempt to wake him up.

The police felt that this might well be closer to the truth, but informed Pate that the injuries observed on the body did not fit this scenario. Finally, at 10 a.m., Pate made a third statement in which he admitted that when Lindesey had fallen to the floor he had just 'cracked up', stood on Lindesey's body, and banged down on him with his fists. As a result, Pate appeared in court later that same day, before the High Bailiff, Mr Weldon Williams, charged with murder.

On 8 April, the postmortem was performed by Dr Joseph

Deguara, at Noble's Hospital. He found eleven broken bones and a ruptured liver, and concluded that there had been a number of heavy blows to the body and chest.

These injuries, he said, would require proper forensic examination, so on 9 April a second postmortem was performed by a Home Office consultant pathologist, Dr Brian Beeson. He discovered that the injuries inflicted upon Lindesey had caused his liver to split in two.

The inquest on Lindesey opened on Wednesday, 22 April, before the coroner, Mr Henry Callow, at Castletown. Basic details of Lindesey's history were given, along with the fact that he had lived in the Ballawoods Gatehouse for many years and had originally operated the railway crossing there for the Isle of Man Railway Company and, since 1978, for the Government Railway Board.

William Thomas Moore gave evidence of identification, confirming that he had known Lindesey for some twenty years and that they had worked together at the White City Amusements, at Onchan, during the evenings.

Medical evidence was given by Dr Jackson and Dr Beeson, after which Patrick Crawford Lindesey took the stand. He told the court that he was a teacher from Llantwit Major and was a nephew of the dead man. He confirmed some of Richard Lindesey's history, but added that Richard had been a rather untidy man with a weak character. He was known to have made friends from the lower social orders and was generous to young men he befriended.

The final witness was Detective Inspector Alan Jones, who stated that a man was in custody and had been charged with murder. The proceedings were then adjourned.

As far as the police investigation was concerned, various court remands followed – including ones on 28 April and 6 May. It was not until June that committal proceedings were concluded, and Pate's trial proper did not start until Tuesday, 29 September.

The trial, before Deemster Corrin, would last until 5

October during which Pate was defended by Mr Geoffrey Karran. The case for the prosecution was detailed by Mr Michael Moyle, and Pate also faced (in addition to the charge of murder) one of larceny in that he had stolen a wallet and a calculator from Lindesey.

Mark Robert Trafford lived in Peel Road, Douglas, and had known Pate for six months. He knew that Pate lived with a man at Ballasalla and believed that he was Pate's grandfather. This was not actually the case, and indeed Pate was not related to Lindesey in any way.

Trafford had met Pate at 7 p.m. on Friday, 3 April 1981, and they went to the Shakespeare Hotel until 8.15 p.m. Later that night they went to the Casino, and in all Pate spent about £20. Trafford thought this strange as he was unemployed at the time.

On the Saturday, the two men returned to the Casino where Pate spent another £20, later giving Trafford a lift home in a car. They met again on Sunday, the 5th, at 6 p.m. when they went together to visit Pate's mother who lived in Ramsey. Later they returned to the Casino where they met up with Malcolm Camp, and the three remained together until 5 a.m. when Trafford was again given a lift home. As far as he knew, the other two had then gone on to Camp's house at Onchan.

This latter part of the evidence was confirmed by Michael Camp. Pate had left his house at 6.15 a.m., saying he was going home to Ballasalla to get some items to sell in a second-hand shop. He had mentioned a television and a tumble dryer. Pate came back to Camp's house in Onchan later that day, but Camp left him there alone as he had to go to work.

Camp got home from work at some time around 2.30 p.m. He was with Pate when he visited a second-hand shop in Windsor Road and sold the items he had mentioned, for which he received £20. They then returned to Camp's house where Camp fell asleep. When he woke, Pate had gone.

Edwin Camp confirmed that Pate had asked him if he might sleep at the house in the early hours of Saturday, 4 April, and he agreed. Edwin went on to tell the story of seeing Pate at his house again at 1.30 a.m. on 6 April when he told him that he had found his grandfather dead and it looked as if he might have been murdered. This was a curious statement since, when Dr Jackson had first examined the body in situ, he had seen no outward signs of violence.

John Ramsey Houghton was able to shed light on what had happened to the property allegedly stolen from the gatehouse. On 6 April 1981, Houghton left his home in Hillberry Road, Onchan, to cycle to work. He noticed a black wallet on the pavement. There was a credit card inside the wallet in the name of R. O. Lindesey. Some hundred yards further down the road, Mr Houghton also found a pocket calculator.

On the third day of the trial, Pate stepped into the witness box to tell his own story. He told the court that his parents had split up when he was just five years old. He went to live with his father and the new woman in his life, but he was often beaten by both of them, sometimes with a leather strap. The family lived in Foxdale at the time and occasionally he had been forced to depend on other people in the area even to feed him. By the time he turned seventeen, he had still not been given a key to the house and was often locked out. On such occasions he had to sleep in a field or in someone's garden.

Pate confirmed that he had first met Robert Lindesey at the gatehouse when he was fourteen years old. He had run away from home after one beating from his father and taken shelter in Lindesey's garage. The old man had found him, taken him into the house, and given him something to eat and drink. Later he showed Pate to the bedroom and told him that he was welcome to stay, but there was only one bed. It was a simple choice. If Pate wanted to stay there, he would have to sleep in the same bed as Lindesey. Pate agreed and they went to bed together, but during the night Lindesey made sexual advances towards him. Pate told him to stop and Lindesey did, and two or three days later the police called and took Pate back to live with his father.

This part of Pate's testimony had, in part, been confirmed by the evidence of Detective Constable Geoffrey Allen who had said that in January 1975 Lindesey had been fined £20 for indecently assaulting Pate.

Continuing his own testimony, Pate said that he had then been in a foster home for three months, but finally returned to his father's house where he stayed until he was seventeen. Previously, his father had told him that his real mother had died, but now Pate discovered that she was alive and living in Ramsey. He then moved in with her and lived quite happily for two years, but then was told that there was not enough room and he was forced to move out.

It was during the two years that he spent living with his mother that Pate had met up with Lindesey again. The two became friends and Lindesey gave him money and alcohol and even took him for rides around the island in his car. In time, Pate came to look upon him as his second father.

It was during this time that Pate went to live in Douglas, but he was unemployed and had money problems. To take his mind off things, he began to sniff glue and take Valium and this led to further problems that culminated in a split from his girlfriend. In due course he met Lindesey again and moved in with him at the gatehouse.

Turning to Friday, 3 April 1981, Pate repeated his story of Lindesey making sexual advances towards him and how he pushed Lindesey away. An argument had started and at one stage Lindesey had picked up a spade and tried to attack him with it. This had caused Pate to lose his temper and he had struck out in anger. Pate also claimed that he had been taking drugs at the time and this had affected his mind.

In his summing up for the defence, Mr Karran reminded the jury that in the Isle of Man it was still an offence to be homosexual. Consequently, the advances made by Lindesey would amount to an indecent assault and that, in turn, could be viewed as provocation.

For the prosecution, Mr Moyle asked if a reasonable person

would kick and trample upon an elderly man, even if provoked, and asked the jury to return a verdict of guilty of murder.

During his own summation, Deemster Corrin informed the jury that if they believed Pate's story of defending himself and that he had not known what he was doing due to the effects of drugs he had taken, then they could return a verdict of manslaughter.

The jury were out for one hour and ten minutes before returning to say that they had found Pate guilty on both counts: murder and theft. Deemster Corrin then sentenced Pate to death on the charge of murder and six months' imprisonment on the charge of larceny. In due course, that death sentence was, as expected, commuted to one of life imprisonment.

14

In Self-defence

Constable Paul John Davenport was on control room duty at the Douglas police headquarters in the early hours of Thursday, 4 February 1982, when – at 12.50 a.m. – an emergency call was put through to him.

The caller identified himself as 29-year-old Graham Samson of Glen View Bungalow, Main Road, Foxdale, and he explained that he and his wife, Rosemary, had argued. Samson went on to say that his wife had hit him with a poker and stabbed him. He had retaliated by pushing her away and the next thing he knew was that she was lying on the floor and wasn't moving.

At 1.05 a.m., Constable Mark Pendlebury, who was based at Port St Mary, arrived at the house. Some forty minutes after this, Dr Roger Harry Ritson, the deputy police surgeon for Douglas, arrived and confirmed that 31-year-old Rosemary Samson, a mother of three, was dead. The doctor also examined Graham Samson and noted that he appeared to be in a semi-stupor. Indeed, the doctor would later report that he had seldom seen such a state of shock exhibited by an individual, and would add that such signs were extremely difficult to fake.

Graham Samson was taken into custody and charged with his wife's murder. He made his first appearance in court later that same day. The proceedings lasted for just five minutes during which the details of the arrest were given. After this, Samson was remanded to Friday, 12 February.

On that same Friday, the inquest on Rosemary opened in Peel before the coroner, Mr Weldon Williams, and a seven-man jury. Those proceedings too were adjourned. Later, Samson made his second court appearance and was remanded for a further week. Eventually, committal proceedings opened, on Thursday, 1 April.

Normally, such a hearing would have been widely reported, but that very day the Criminal Law Act had come into force and this severely limited the reporting of criminal proceedings. In fact, little information was printed beyond the fact that Samson was represented by Mr John Crellin and Mr Peter Wood. Finally, however, after a hearing lasting three days, Samson was sent for trial, on Tuesday, 6 April.

Samson's trial for murder opened on Tuesday, 13 July, before Deemster Corrin and a jury of nine men and three women. The hearing was to last for one week.

Dr Brian Beeson, a Home Office pathologist, had examined Samson at the Douglas police headquarters on 4 February. He noted cuts and puncture marks on the prisoner's arms, but added that these were very regular and controlled and there was a possibility that they had been self-inflicted. Dr Beeson had also examined Rosemary and stated that she had been stabbed four times. All the wounds were in her chest, and one of them had penetrated her heart and was the immediate cause of death.

Thomas James Briggs from the Home Office North West Science Laboratory at Chorley had also visited the house at Foxdale on 4 February. He reported two areas of bloodstaining on the kitchen floor and of finding two bloodstained knives. Tests had shown that blood on one of the knives could have come from Rosemary but not from Graham and, on the other knife, the blood could have come from Graham but not from Rosemary. The conclusion was, of course, that each of the knives had been used on each of the protagonists; though this of itself did not prove that Rosemary had wielded one of them, fingerprint evidence was able to confirm this.

Samson's own story was then told in court. He related how he had undergone some treatment at the Ballamona Hospital for certain matrimonial problems and that this had caused strain in his relationship with Rosemary. Indeed, at one stage she had left him for a short time.

Samson continued by saying that he had been born in Chesham, Buckinghamshire. He had travelled to the Isle of Man originally to watch the TT Races some ten years before and that was how he had first met Rosemary and they had fallen in love and married. Now he worked as a setter/operator with the Ronaldsway Airport Company. On Wednesday, 3 February, he had arrived home from work at 5.45 p.m. only to find his wife getting ready to go out. When he politely asked her where she was going she replied, 'None of your business.'

Rosemary returned to the house at around 11 p.m. and he asked if they could go out together, as a couple, on the coming Saturday. Rosemary replied that she had already made arrangements to go out with Bev Wilkinson and some other friends, and an argument then ensued when he commented that her friends seemed to be more important to her than he was.

As the argument continued, Rosemary became more and more abusive and then started to slap him. In retaliation he slapped her back and she pushed him. Samson had not wanted any confrontation, so walked into the kitchen to get away from her. She followed him, carrying a knife, and now she started prodding him with it, saying that she wanted to get rid of him.

Samson continued, 'I knew she wanted to hurt me. I thought she wanted to kill me. She kept coming and I pushed her away.' Rosemary finally backed him into a corner and it was now, he said, that instinct took over. Without realizing what was happening, he picked up a knife and defended himself. Samson freely admitted that he was responsible for Rosemary's death but that it was a case of self-defence.

Samson's testimony was in part backed up by other witnesses. Ada Cubbon ran the Glen View Stores which was next door to Samson's bungalow. They had last been into her shop the day before Rosemary's death – Wednesday, 3

February. They seemed to be a nice, happy couple and Samson had always treated his wife well.

Joan Mary Elsinger, a part-time art teacher, knew the couple very well and had done ever since Samson first came to the island. She stated that they seemed to be very happy together until February. Around that time, Samson seemed not to be his old self. Joan added that she thought that Rosemary had an almost bewitching influence over her husband.

Susan Margaret O'Hanlon, another family friend, gave the simple statement that in her opinion Samson loved Rosemary, but she didn't love him in return. Finally, other witnesses testified that Rosemary had certainly been the dominant partner.

In his summing up, which lasted for two hours, Deemster Corrin said, 'A person who acted in reasonable self-defence should be found not guilty of murder, and if a person was provoked into causing a death the jury should reduce the murder charge to manslaughter.'

The jury were out for two and a half hours and when they returned they announced that they had found Samson not guilty. At this, a woman in the public gallery shouted out in disbelief and had to be led from the court. Moments later, Deemster Corrin told Samson that he was free to go.

15

The Babysitter

In 1979, Clodi Battista, an Italian national then aged just twenty, came to live on the Isle of Man. Soon after this she found herself pregnant and, on 30 November 1980, gave birth to a baby boy whom she named Brian Marcus. The father of the child by now had nothing to do with Miss Battista and left the island soon afterwards.

By the time she was twenty-one, in 1981, Clodi Battista had become involved with an 18-year-old man named Stephen Philip Moore and in due course the three of them moved into a first-floor flat in Bucks Road, Douglas. There were, however, some problems to concern this new family group.

To begin with, Moore was unemployed so the only real money coming into the household were the wages Clodi earned as a barmaid in a local public house. There was also the fact that it was clear that Moore didn't much like baby Brian – and Brian, in turn, was not enamoured of the new man in his mother's life.

In due course, Clodi found herself pregnant again and she and Moore discussed marriage. They finally agreed on a date; they would tie the knot on 29 April 1982. Before that date, however, something was to happen that would change everything, for ever.

There had always been frequent arguments between Moore and Clodi. Sometimes, Moore lost his temper with the baby and hit out at him, though he always seemed to be sorry afterwards. On one occasion, though, Moore hit Brian so hard that he left bruises on the child's buttocks and Clodi's mother called the police. Clodi herself packed Moore's bags for him and left them near the front door. She told him to clear off, but Moore returned later and was allowed to stay.

The usual routine now was that Clodi would go to work at the bar, leaving Brian in the care of Moore. It wasn't an ideal solution, but felt she had no other choice. She had to earn money to support herself and Brian. Things were no different on 20 April 1982. Clodi left for work at around noon, leaving Brian with Moore. She did not return home until just after 5 p.m., having taken some ten minutes to walk back from the bar. Moore was sitting on the settee, watching television, and informed her that Brian was asleep in bed. Clodi did go to check on the boy and found him rather cold, but thought nothing more about it.

Going back into the living room, another argument began between Clodi and Moore when she accused him of spending money they could ill afford. As the row escalated, Clodi threw a book at Moore, followed soon afterwards by a clock. He would later claim that she attacked him but, whatever the truth of that, Clodi demanded that he leave the flat. Moore did so, shouting back that he was 'Going for good'.

For some thirty minutes after Moore had left, Clodi busied herself tidying up the flat. She then saw that it was about time to feed Brian and left, very briefly, to go to a local shop. Upon her return she prepared Brian's food and then went to wake the child. To her horror, Clodi found that she could not rouse him. She panicked and began screaming, a noise that was heard by Elaine Gordon, a neighbour from the third floor who happened to be sitting on the front doorstep, waiting for her boyfriend to arrive. Elaine ran upstairs to see what the matter was.

Clodi was holding Brian and still shouting hysterically. Elaine advised Clodi to take the child to hospital, and together the two women dashed to the nearby Noble's Hospital. Elaine would later say that even though she mentioned nothing to Clodi, she knew on that journey the Brian was already dead.

At the hospital's Accident and Emergency department,

Brian was handed over to Dr Fay Rennie who confirmed that the baby was indeed dead. Soon after this, Clodi was allowed to view the body. The child had by now been stripped and, for the first time, Clodi noticed the bruises over much of his body. Later still, she returned to her flat in Bucks Road.

Moore, meanwhile, had gone into Douglas and met up with a friend of his, Forbes Ivor Donovan, at around 7.30 p.m. The two men decided on a game of snooker, but first they went to the same bar where Clodi was employed as a barmaid. It was in that bar that Moore learned that Brian had been taken to the hospital, but he seemed to show no interest in that news and carried on with his game of snooker. In Donovan's opinion, though, Moore did appear rather quieter than usual but Donovan put this down to Moore's announcement that he had been thrown out of the flat after yet another row. As for Brian, Moore said during the evening that he loved the child and added that he had been 'really good' while he looked after him.

At 10.30 p.m., Moore returned to the flat in Bucks Road. Naturally, he was questioned by Clodi after she had informed him that Brian was dead, but Moore denied harming the child in any way. Soon after this, though, the police arrived and both Moore and Clodi were taken to the station. It was there that for the first time, according to Clodi, Moore admitted that he had hit Brian.

Clodi was allowed to go home first. The following morning, 21 April, Moore arrived back at the flat and again denied beating Brian. At the same time, Dr Joseph Deguala, a consultant pathologist at Noble's Hospital, was performing a postmortem on Brian Battista. Dr Deguala soon discovered that death did not appear to have been due to natural causes and called in Dr Brain Beeson, a forensic pathologist, to make his own examination. Dr Beeson flew over to the island and, when he completed his own postmortem, determined that Brian's bruises were compatible with blows from a fist and had probably been caused by the knuckles of a hand. The blows had been delivered with some force, probably as the boy lay up against a hard surface, and had caused a split in the liver. The child had bled to death from the injury to his liver.

It was also on 21 April that Moore was interviewed again. Faced with the medical findings, Moore now admitted that he might have been responsible for Brian's death, but stressed that it had been an accident. He had been playing with Brian and bouncing him high on his knee. Suddenly his left knee accidentally struck Brian in the stomach, causing him to cry out in pain, but he soon calmed down after fifteen minutes or so and Moore had not thought he had been badly hurt.

The interviews continued and in due course Moore told a slightly different story to Detective Constable Andrew Bullock. Now Moore said he had been on the bed with Brian, straddling the child and playing with him. He had been bouncing on the bed quite high and at one stage his attention had been distracted and had glanced out of the window into the street below. As he came down, he had caught Brian in the stomach with his knee and this must have caused the injury. He had not thought the child to be badly hurt and indeed, after crying for a short time, Brian had settled down so Moore had put him to bed to allow him to sleep. Constable Bullock told Moore that he just did not believe him and finally, at lunchtime on 22 April, Moore admitted that he had punched Brian but added, 'At no time did I want to hurt him or kill him.' Moore was then charged with murder.

Moore's trial opened on Monday, 22 November 1982, before Deemster Corrin. The prosecution case was put by Mr Michael Moyle, while Moore was defended by Mr Robert Jelski. The proceedings would last for eight days until Wednesday, 1 December.

Further evidence was given of the way Moore had treated Brian Battista. Hugh Oliver was the manager of an amusement arcade in Strand Street and he had seen Moore in there a number of times, occasionally with Brian. Hugh had spoken to Moore several times about the way he was treating the baby.

On one occasion he had seen Moore playing pool. He had put the baby underneath the table and was holding Brian still by placing his foot on the boy's head. On another occasion he had seen Moore hit Brian very violently.

Evidence was given that Moore had made three statements to the police. In the first, to Constable Mike Cowell, he had completely denied causing any injury to Brian. In the second, he admitted that the injury might have been caused accidentally in play, and in the third, he admitted punching Brian in the abdomen. Apparently he had been trying to put a fresh nappy on to Brian, but the boy had been playing up so eventually Moore had lost his temper and hit Brian.

Now, in court, Moore was making fresh allegations. He had only made the second statement because the police had said that if he did he would then be allowed to see a lawyer. As for the third statement, he had only signed this because he had been beaten up by police officers.

The jury of ten men and two women retired to consider their verdict on 1 December, and after one hour returned to state that they had found Moore guilty of murder. He was then sentenced to death. On hearing this, Moore replied that he wished to appeal.

The death sentence was, of course, commuted to a sentence of life imprisonment by the Home Secretary of the time, William Whitelaw. Moore did indeed appeal against the verdict and that appeal was heard, and rejected in February 1983, as was an appeal to the Privy Council in March 1987 whereupon Moore was sent back to jail to serve out the rest of his sentence.

16

The Contract Killer

Pamela Hopkinson was most concerned. She had last spoken to her daughter, 21-year-old Corinne Bentley, on Thursday, 11 July 1991. Their telephone calls were a regular thing, with Pamela ringing Corinne each Thursday. There had been no reply on 18 July, so the next day – Friday, 19 July – Pamela rang the police and reported her daughter as a missing person. Coincidentally, that Friday was Corinne's twenty-second birthday.

Corinne Bentley had been born to William and Pamela Bentley, in Lancashire, on 19 July 1969. Her parents had divorced when she was just five years old and both had subsequently remarried. After the divorce, Corinne had stayed with her mother. Pamela had married Peter Hopkinson in 1980 and some eight years later, in June 1988, the family moved to the Isle of Man and ran an amusement centre on the seafront at Ramsey. As Corinne grew older she took several jobs on the island, including working at the Grand Island Hotel but finally, in September 1989, she found full-time employment at the Home of Rest in Ramsey. Two years after this, in June 1991, Corinne's mother and step-father sold the business and moved back to Lancashire. Corinne stayed behind on the island. After all, she was making something of her life now and had made some good friends. In short, she was a happy girl with everything to live for. She was certainly not the type of girl simply to go missing.

Soon after Corinne had been reported as a missing person, a description of her appeared in the Manx newspapers.

Corinne was reported as being 5 feet 2 inches tall, of slim build, with hazel eyes, and shoulder-length mousy-coloured hair. It was also reported that although she was now twenty-two years old, she was rather slow for her age and behaved like a sixteen-year-old.

The initial police investigation showed that of late Corinne had been sleeping rough in bus shelters and the like. She had also started a relationship with a man named Elliot Dickson Kinvig who lived at Lhergy Farm, St Mark's. In fact, Elliott owned Lhergy Farm, having been left it in his father's will. Also living there were Elliot's mother, sister and his sister's common-law husband, Anthony Nicholas Burrows, though the atmosphere was perhaps not all that it should have been as there had been a recent family argument and Elliott had even threatened to throw the others out.

When Elliott Kinvig was interviewed he reported that he had last seen Corinne on the evening of Thursday, 11 July. Elliott recalled that it had been a rainy night and he and Corinne had been offered a lift home from the local pub by a man driving a green Mini. In due course, Elliott had been dropped off, but the driver had told Corinne that he knew a man in the north of the island who might be able to offer her work. She had expressed interest and Elliott had then watched them drive off together. Elliott was then able to give a few more details of the vehicle adding that it had yellow wheels, letters on the bonnet, and orange-coloured clothes pegs attached to the clutch. He was also able to give a description of the driver.

It was a relatively simple matter to trace such a distinctive vehicle and records showed that it was registered to Sharon Culshaw, a bank secretary. She in turn was able to say that the car was often used by her fiancé, Anthony Robin Denys Teare.

Anthony Teare lived with his parents, Denys and Faye, in Ormly Avenue, Ramsey. His father, Denys, was a best-selling author who had come to the island in the late 1960s. They had started by operating a quayside market in Ramsey, but had to give that up when Faye's health failed a little. Denys had then taken to writing and had published three books. As for Anthony, he had been a marshal at the TT races and now worked for a refrigeration company.

In due course, Teare walked voluntarily into the police station, and claimed that he did not know Corinne Bentley and also knew nothing of her disappearance. It was now Tuesday, 23 July 1991, and Corinne had been missing for twelve days.

Things moved rapidly from then on. The green Mini with yellow wheels was by now parked at the police headquarters and it was there that Elliott Kinvig positively identified it as the vehicle he had seen. Tests on the car showed the presence of bloodstains and, consequently, Teare was interviewed at length by Detective Sergeant David Hastie and Detective Constable David Fletcher. Finally, Teare broke down and confessed that he was responsible for Corinne's death, saying, 'I'm going to be in a lot of trouble for this. I took her out to Ballaugh and she never came back.'

Teare went on to admit that he had slashed Corinne's throat, several times, with a Stanley knife and then offered to take officers to where they would find her body. Sergeant Hastie then passed all the information on to Detective Inspector Robert Walls and the three officers, Walls, Hastie and Fletcher, then drove Teare out to a quiet lane leading to Druidale Farm near Sulby reservoir. Teare indicated exactly where the attack had taken place but refused to get out of the car, claiming that he didn't want to see Corinne's body. There was no immediate sign of a body, so dozens of police officers were drafted in to search the area while Teare was driven back to the police station where he made a full written statement. It made chilling reading and indicated that this was a contract killing.

Teare was employed as an apprentice electrician and one of the people he worked with was Anthony Burrows, the man who lived at Lhergy Farm with Elliott Kinvig and his family. According to Teare, Burrows was concerned about the possibility that Elliott was about to move Corinne into the farm and this might cost him his home. He had discussed this with Teare, and at one stage had made the comment that he wanted her 'bumped off'.

The conversation continued and Burrows seemed to imply that he would pay someone to do the deed for him. Teare had then asked how much this might cost and was surprised to hear Burrows say that it would be about £600. He told his friend that he had thought it might cost thousands and then added, jokingly, that he would do it for £200. Teare stressed that he thought this was all a wind-up, but some days later they had talked about it again and Burrows had said, 'Send Elliott her head. That would upset him.'

Teare now took the situation more seriously and, acting on what he believed were instructions, had driven Corinne out to the lonely lane where he had pulled over, pretending to run out of petrol. Once Corinne was off her guard he had taken out his Stanley knife, slashed her throat, and then dumped her body in a hedge. The following day he had shown a bloodstained blanket to Burrows and told him that he had killed Corinne. He had even pointed out, on a map of the island, where he had committed the crime. Burrows was genuinely shocked and said, 'You're a bloody fool if you have done', and then said he didn't want to know any more in case he was implicated. As for the motive for this murder, Teare had wanted the £200 to pay off his bank overdraft which was worrying him – even though it stood at just £8 on the day Corinne had gone missing.

Teare was charged with murder on the evening of Tuesday, 23 July 1991. Later still, Anthony Burrows was arrested and charged with offering to obtain £200 for Teare, knowing or believing him to have committed an arrestable offence. Meanwhile, the search for Corinne's body continued.

The next day, Wednesday, 24 July, Constable Raymond Michael Radcliffe was part of the police team searching the area around Druidale Farm when he spotted what appeared to be a mound of rubble close by a disused silage channel. Moving closer, he saw a training shoe and then part of a human leg. Finally, Corinne Bentley, a girl who had never reached her twenty-second birthday, had been found.

Corinne's body was very badly decomposed. Much of her face and hands had been attacked by rodents and there was extensive maggot infestation. As a result, it fell to her dentist, Peter Coombe, who had a practice at Ramsey, to make the final identification. He had treated Corinne between December 1988 and January 1989, and examined the body at 9 p.m. that same Wednesday. He was able to confirm that the fillings, cavities and wisdom teeth showed without any doubt that the body was that of Corinne.

On Thursday, 25 July, Teare made the first of a number of court appearances before the Deputy High Bailiff, Andrew Williamson, where evidence of arrest was given. That same day, the inquest on Corinne opened and the evidence of identification given. Those proceedings were then adjourned until Tuesday, 27 August, when medical evidence on Corinne's injuries was given before the inquest was adjourned indefinitely, pending the outcome of the criminal trial.

That trial, the first for murder in ten years, opened on Monday, 28 June 1992, before Deemster Henry Callow and a jury of six men and six women. Teare's defence lay in the hands of Mr Robert Jelski, while the case for the prosecution was detailed by Mr Michael Moyle.

Evidence was given that showed that after Corinne had been attacked and left for dead, she had actually managed to stagger a hundred yards or so, towards Druidale Farm, probably seeking help. She had then succumbed to her injuries and fallen into the drain where she had ultimately been found.

This particular piece of evidence was significant at the time and would prove to be of even more significance later, for another witness was Joan Desprez who operated part of Druidale Farm. She was first interviewed by the police on 23 July 1991, the day before Corinne's body was discovered. She told officers that on Friday, 12 July, the day after Corinne had been attacked, she had found a patch of blood in the stable yard, and another, larger patch in the driveway leading up to the farm. At the time, Joan believed that the blood had come from a pheasant that had gone missing and she assumed had probably been taken by a fox. There was, however, something else – which Joan had missed.

Once the police had interviewed Joan, they began searching in the area where she said she had seen blood. Officers found an ear-ring which had belonged to Corinne, showing that this was the area where she had first been attacked, lost the ear-ring, and then staggered on towards the farm buildings. Joan explained that she might well have missed this vital clue because the pool of blood was rather thick and may well have obscured it.

On the third day of the trial, Wednesday, 1 July, the proceedings had to be halted as Dr Anthony Davidson, the Home Office pathologist, was on holiday and so not able to give evidence. He had not been informed that the trial was under way and, as a result, matters had to be adjourned for a full week, recommencing on Wednesday, 8 July.

All the evidence having been heard, the jury retired on Friday, 10 July 1992, and when they returned to court, announced that they had found Teare guilty of murder. Deemster Callow then passed the last ever death sentence in the United Kingdom. Teare was told that he had twenty-eight days to appeal against the sentence.

An appeal was indeed entered and, on 13 October, Teare's defence applied to the court to appoint an expert criminal barrister. Despite protestations from Teare's parents, Faye and Denys, Lieutenant Governor Sir Lawrence Jones refused permission on the grounds that the case was straightforward and well within the capabilities of members of the Manx bar. However, the case was to prove far from straightforward because new evidence had now been revealed.

In due course it was decided that this new evidence would have to be tested in open court. As a result, on Monday, 15 November 1993, Deemster Corrin and acting Deemster

Hytner sat to decide the issue of Teare's conviction. By now Teare had obtained new representation in the form of Mr Peter Thornton and he argued that there were grounds for declaring the conviction unsafe and unsatisfactory. The two deemsters agreed and Teare's conviction was quashed. He would have to face an entirely new trial.

Teare's new trial opened on Wednesday, 13 April 1994, before the acting deemster, Brian Leveson. The prosecution was led by Mr Clement Goldstone, assisted by Mr Alastair Montgomerie, while Teare was defended by Mr Peter Thornton, assisted by Ms Louise Byrne. The proceedings would last for ten days.

In fact, the first day and a half of the proceedings were heard without a jury as the Deemster listened to legal arguments from both sides over whether Teare's original confession was admissible or not. Finally it was decided that it was, and a jury of six men and six women sworn in.

There were a number of reasons for this second trial and, in addition to all the previous witnesses, a number of new points were raised. The first of these was connected with Detective Sergeant David Hastie, one of the first officers to interview Teare in 1991.

Teare was now claiming that he had been denied his basic rights and had only confessed to the murder when he had been told, 'There's no way you're leaving this place until we find out what's happened.' Sergeant Hastie denied ever making this threat. He also denied copying a colleague's notes as to what had happened. The inference was that Sergeant Hastie had copied notes from Constable Fletcher.

Another issue was the blood found in the green Mini in which the prosecution said the attack had taken place. All that could be said was that there were two types found in the vehicle and these were 'consistent' with the defendant's and the victim's. In short, two types of blood had been discovered, but they could not positively be identified as either Corinne's or Teare's.

Then there was the identification made by Elliott Kinvig, Corinne's boyfriend. He had indeed identified the green Mini, but had failed to pick out Teare in court. Just like Corinne, Elliott was described as educationally slow and it was held that his identification evidence was consequently unsafe.

Finally, there was the evidence of the blood pools at Druidale Farm, described by Joan Desprez. Originally she had claimed that she had seen these on Friday, 12 July, but part of her statement had described how she had pinned down this day by saying that she had been going to check some hay to see if it was dry enough to bale. The night Corinne had last been seen alive was a rainy day and the first dry day afterwards was Sunday, 14 July. The inference was that Joan had seen the blood pools on that date meaning that Corinne was alive after 11 July when Elliott Kinvig had last seen her.

The verdict came on Tuesday, 26 April 1994, and again the jury decided that Teare was guilty of murder. Just as he had entered the history books as the last man ever to be awarded a death sentence, Teare now gained another distinction as the first person on the Isle of Man to get the now mandatory sentence of life imprisonment – with Deemster Leveson imposing a minimum term of twelve years.

For Corinne Bentley, it was all of no importance. Her life had been taken for no real reason, just as she faced a future filled with hope and possibilities.

17

Rave Night

In 1993, a new nightclub opened on the promenade at Douglas. Based around an Elton John theme, the club, known as EJ's, formed part of the Hotel Continental site on the Queen's Promenade. After a year, though, there were various problems connected with the lease, and the management decided that introducing rave nights might be one possible solution. Several such events were organized and seemed to go relatively well, until the evening of Friday, 30 September 1994.

On that Friday there were around 350 people in EJ's, and only two – somewhat inexperienced – doormen supervising the entrance. Neal Clague was the DJ on duty, and as Friday passed on into Saturday, 1 October, it looked like it was going to be another uneventful night for him and the rest of the staff. Then, at around 1.15 a.m., everything changed.

Suddenly there were hysterical people around the foyer and a policeman had to tell Neal Clague to switch the music off. People were prevented from leaving the club until officers had spoken to them, though around twenty had actually left before the police arrived. The reason for this sudden police activity could be found in the foyer and on the promenade outside. A total of four young men had been attacked and one was now fighting for his life.

Peter Michel Raby had been badly beaten and had suffered extensive bruising to the front of his chest. His cousin, Colin Bernard Raby, had been stabbed in the neck. A friend, David Joseph Steventon, had been stabbed twice, once in the abdomen and once in the right eye. Meanwhile, 18-year-old Steven Helwich of Hawarden Avenue, Douglas, had also been stabbed twice, and was lying in a pool of blood on the floor in the foyer, his eyes fixed and staring upwards, his skin white and his lips blue. Medical officers could find no pulse and, despite constant medical intervention in the ambulance, Steven was pronounced dead on arrival at the hospital.

The first two police officers on the scene had been Constable Alan Chambers and Constable Ian MacDonald who were patrolling the promenade in a police van when one of the doormen at EJ's flagged them down. They had found Steven Helwich lying on the floor, a pool of blood underneath his head, and David Steventon standing nearby, bleeding profusely from the region of his right eye. It was Constable Chambers who radioed through to his headquarters for assistance and also asked that an ambulance be sent immediately. Even before that ambulance arrived, another police officer, Detective Constable Gary Roberts, arrived at the nightclub and it was he who took Colin Raby across the road. Colin was obviously in pain.

The ambulance arrived with Tracy Carolyn Harvey and Graham Michael Skinner in attendance. By now a large crowd of people had gathered outside the club and it was with a great deal of difficulty that Tracy and Graham manhandled a trolley through the crowd so that they could load Steven Helwich, the most severely injured man, into the ambulance. On the way to the hospital, Tracy Harvey manually ventilated Steven while her partner radioed ahead for a crash team to be ready. It was all to no avail and, after Steven had been left at the hospital, Tracy and Graham returned to the Queen's Promenade and the nightclub.

The next casualty they dealt with was Colin Raby, who by now was leaning over the railings opposite the club. His shirt was heavily soaked in blood and Colin had been sick. That may have been due to the fact that he had been drinking, but also might have been as a result of shock. Colin didn't seem to be fully aware of the injuries he had received and Tracy saw that he had a triangular-shaped hole in his neck.

The police meanwhile had entered the club premises and what they found shocked them. The floor inside was littered with very small plastic bags. Each of them had contained a single Ecstasy tablet which had changed hands during the night for up to £20 per pill. Outside the premises, a quantity of knives had been found, no doubt dropped by some of the clientele before they could be spoken to or searched by officers. Although all of these were later tested, none were found to have been used in the attacks. Inquiries had, however, given the police a name. Witnesses, including Amanda Byron who had been standing just feet away from the stabbing, had named the culprit as Charles McCluskey.

In fact, McCluskey had gone to EJ's that night with two companions: 19-year-old Michael Gardner and Jim Nolan, a Scot who had only arrived on the island on Friday, 30 September. It now became clear that Peter Raby had been the first man to be attacked, having been thrown to the ground and kicked by three men in the toilets. The other three had been attacked and stabbed soon afterwards.

Inquiries continued and it soon became clear that a young lady named Katherine Corrin was an ex-girlfriend of Michael Gardner. She was duly traced to an address in Malew Street, Castletown, and it was there, at around 2.30 a.m. on that same Saturday morning, that Jim Nolan was arrested. Other occupants of the flat were interviewed, including Miss Corrin herself, who admitted that she had driven the three men away from the nightclub. Once they were at Malew Street, McCluskey had asked her to check him for bloodstains. Unfortunately, the other two men had now moved on and an island-wide manhunt was launched for them.

In fact, McCluskey and Gardner had checked into the Stanleyville Guest House in Ramsey, using the false name of Stevenson and giving a home address at Friary Park, Ballabeg. The house was run by Michael George Gillings and his wife,

Sandra, who noticed nothing unusual about the two young men. One of them seemed to be particularly polite, especially when he purchased a silver Ford Sierra from Paul Frederick Mylchreest who lived next door to the Gillings.

Diligent police work led to that car being identified, and by Monday, 3 October, police throughout the island were on the lookout for it. At 7 p.m. that evening, Detective Constable Toby Patrick Neale was driving an unmarked police car when the silver Ford passed him travelling in the opposite direction. Constable Neale did an immediate U-turn and, keeping a safe distance, radioed through his location to his headquarters. The officer kept up a running commentary and was informed that a road-block had now been set up ahead of them, at the entrance to the Bradda View estate. In due course, the Ford stopped at the road-block and Constable Neale drove his own vehicle close behind the Ford in order to prevent an escape.

Two officers, David Ivor Henry Wood and James Scully, now approached the silver Ford and identified themselves as armed police officers. The two occupants of the car were ordered to get out and lie down on the ground; this they did, without offering any resistance. McCluskey had been sitting in the front passenger seat and, told that he was being arrested on a charge of murder, merely answered, 'Aye, I understand.'

Charles McCluskey, twenty-eight, appeared in court to answer that charge of murder on Monday, 30 October 1995, before Deemster William Cain and a jury of eight men and four women. In all, McCluskey faced three charges. In addition to the murder of Steven Helwich, he was also charged with the attempted murder of David Steventon and also of assaulting Peter Raby. McCluskey's defence lay in the hands of Mr Phil Garrett who was assisted by Ms Rosemary Kelly. The case for the prosecution was led by Mr Alastair Montgomerie. The proceedings would last until the following Monday, though this was due, in part, to the defence team having no witnesses available after the prosecution case was completed, earlier than had been expected, on Thursday, 2 November. As a result, the trial had to be adjourned to that final Monday.

Home Office pathologist Dr Edmund Tapp had carried out the postmortem examination on Steven Helwich. He reported two stab wounds. The first of these, inflicted upon Steven's back, had been so forceful that the knife used had penetrated the bone of his shoulder blade. The knife had passed through the muscle in the back of the chest and gone on through the central part of the shoulder blade before entering the chest cavity.

The second wound was even more severe and had been inflicted on the left side of the neck behind the large muscle which ran down from the ear. The knife had gone in some 6 inches and had travelled downwards at a slight angle. One of the main arteries had been cut and the wound had ended as the blade entered the aorta.

On this particular wound, a great deal of force had been applied because the hilt of the weapon used had left bruising around the wound. In short, the knife had been driven in up to the hilt. In Dr Tapp's opinion, Steven would have died within twenty minutes of being attacked.

Dr Christopher Dowman had been working in the casualty department of the hospital and attended all four victims on the morning of the attack. It was Dr Dowman who certified that Steven Helwich was dead on arrival at the hospital. For the defence, Mr Garrett asked Dr Dowman if the wounds inflicted upon David Steventon were similar in nature to those on Steven, the implication being that McCluskey had not attacked both men. Dr Dowman said he was unable to comment. He stated that he had not gone around measuring the wounds as he was too busy attending to the casualties.

The next witness was Mr Nicholas Batey, a consultant surgeon who stated that David Steventon's abdominal wound was not life threatening. Asked if he believed all the various wounds had been inflicted by the same knife, he too was unable to comment.

Dr James Patrick Travers was a consultant eye-surgeon and he gave evidence on the other stab wound inflicted upon David Steventon, the one to his right eye. Dr Travers testified that the eye was perforated and the globe of the eye had been burst. There was a fracture to the socket of the eye and the injury seen was consistent with a downward movement of a knife, rather than some sort of slashing blow. This wound, although most severe, was also not life threatening.

Various blood samples had been taken and sent to England for DNA profiling. Evidence on the results of these tests was given by Mr Jonathan Paul Whitaker, a forensic scientist. He stated that despite blood samples being found in the flat at Malew Street in Castletown, they could not have originated from either Charles McCluskey, Jim Nolan or Michael Gardner. Furthermore, clothing found dumped in Marine Drive and at Langness had also been tested, but the samples failed to yield sufficient DNA for testing. As Deemster Cain explained to the jury, there was, in effect, no forensic evidence in this case.

Detective Sergeant Sydney James Barry had interviewed McCluskey at the police station after his arrest. In his first interview, McCluskey had exercised his right to silence and had not requested legal representation. By the time of his second interview, McCluskey had obtained the service of Mr Garrett who now represented him in court. The police had asked McCluskey to attend an identity parade and he had refused.

For the defence, Mr Garrett now took pains to show that this was not in any way suspicious. Detailed descriptions of the wanted men had been published in the local newspapers and the one of McCluskey was now read out in court. It described him as a Scot, aged twenty-seven, known as Chuck or Chucky, white, 5 feet 11 inches tall, with short black hair, blue eyes, a squint and tattoos on his hand and arm. With such a description, it would have been extremely dangerous for McCluskey to consent to a parade. Questioned in detail about this, Sergeant Barry agreed that a refusal to attend was not unjustified.

All the evidence being heard, the jury retired to consider their verdict. When it came, it was that McCluskey was guilty on all three charges. The court was then adjourned for two weeks before sentencing.

Deemster Cain reconvened the court on Friday, 17 November, and sentenced McCluskey to life imprisonment with a minimum term of fifteen years for the murder of Steven Helwich. He was also sentenced to twelve years for the attempted murder of David Steventon and six months for the assault upon Peter Raby with the sentences to run concurrently. The man who had been arrested with him, Michael Gardner, received two years in prison for assisting McCluskey knowing that he had committed an offence. There were cheers in the court as the sentences were announced.

An appeal against the conviction was launched by McCluskey and dismissed in early 1996. However, a second appeal was launched in May 2003 with McCluskey claiming incompetence on behalf of his defence team. The hearing of this second appeal was originally due to take place in early January 2004, but Mr Brian Higgs, who was now representing McCluskey, argued for an adjournment. The case was finally heard by Judge of Appeal Mr Geoffrey Tattersall in April and lasted for three days, with McCluskey being brought back to the island from his prison in Kilmarnock. This appeal was also rejected.

The tragic case of Steven Helwich did lead to major changes on the Isle of Man. Concerned over the lack of security at such clubs, the law was changed. Criminal record checks were now to be made on any security staff in such establishments and proper training introduced. As for the nightclub where the murder took place, it closed after the attack and was never reopened.

18

The Demon Drink

It had been a most pleasant New Year's Day. Frank and Avril Griffin had started drinking together in the Peel Castle public house. From there, Frank, a retired publican, went on to drink alone in the Creek Inn and then The Marine. Meanwhile, Avril went on her own pub crawl and by the time she went home to 4 Fenella Terrace, Peel, she was staggering. It was then sometime between 11 p.m. and midnight on Wednesday, 1 January 1997.

It was the early hours of 2 January when Frank Griffin fell into bed beside his wife. He was soon in a deep sleep but, by

The Peel Castle Hotel where Frank and Avril Griffin were drinking on 1 January 1997, prior to her death

three o'clock, Frank was in a payphone, calling a family friend, Carol Quayle. Apparently there was something seriously wrong. Frank could not rouse his wife and was desperate for someone to help. Without further delay, Carol Quayle dashed around to Fenella Terrace and what she saw caused her to make her own telephone call from that public call box.

The emergency call to the ambulance headquarters in Douglas was timed at 3.15 a.m. Medical aid was despatched, but it was too late. Avril Griffin was already dead and the police were called to attend. What they found caused Frank Griffin to be taken in by the police for further questioning.

A distraught Frank explained that he and Avril had been married for some five years. Though they had no children of their own, Avril did have five from two previous marriages and a further common-law relationship. Both she and Frank were rather too fond of drink and on such occasions arguments and differences of opinions could cause some friction between them. Frank explained that he had loved his wife dearly but, when she was suffering from the effects of alcohol, he might have to restrain her. He had done this many times during their marriage and this had been one such occasion.

Frank said that he had been asleep in bed when Avril had suddenly attacked him. He was forced, yet again, to restrain her and they struggled for a minute or so. She then fell still and he thought that he had merely subdued her, so her left her on the bed while he went to use the toilet.

Upon his return to the bedroom, Frank saw immediately that there was something wrong. Avril had not moved, but at first Frank thought she was playacting and told her to stop being silly and get into bed. When she failed to respond he gave her the kiss of life, but that didn't work either. That was when he had run to the call box and telephoned Carol Quayle as he didn't know what else to do.

There were, however, two problems with this scenario. To begin with, a spot of blood had been discovered in the centre of Avril's pillow on the bed. The police believed that this was consistent, perhaps, with Avril's face being forced down into the pillow.

There was also the statement given by Ian Howard Baker, a barman at the Marine Hotel in Peel, whose wife had left him some time before. According to Baker's statement, Frank had spoken to him on the evening of 1 January and said, 'You are a lucky bastard. You got rid of your wife ... at least she's fucking gone. I wish I could get rid of mine.' As a result of that statement and the blood evidence, Frank Griffin was arrested and charged with the murder of his wife.

The trial of Frank Griffin opened on Monday, 6 August 1997, before Deemster William Cain. The case for the prosecution was led by Mr Alastair Montgomerie while Griffin was defended by Mr Alan Gough. Griffin pleaded not guilty to murder.

Evidence was given that when the paramedics and the police attended the house in the early hours of 2 January, Avril had been lying fully clothed on the bed, on her back. Her head was at the foot of the bed and her feet were up near the headboard.

Dr Edmund Tapp, a Home Office pathologist, testified that

4 Fenella Terrace, Peel, where Avril Griffin died

there was bruising around Avril's mouth which was consistent with a hand being placed over her mouth, though Griffin denied having done this. There were also impressions and marks inside the mouth which could have been caused by the teeth coming into contact with the lips and cheeks. Scratches found on her face and body could have been caused by an attacker or be defence marks caused as she tried to remove something from her face. In all, Dr Tapp had noted twenty-one injuries to Avril's head and face and a further ten to her body.

It was on the fourth day of the proceedings that the trial, in effect, collapsed. Ian Baker now stated that when Frank was talking to him in the bar he had only expressed a wish that she would leave him. It was now that Mr Gough, for the defence, sought to argue, in the absence of the jury, that other evidence should not be admitted.

The single drop of blood on the pillow had been tested and shown to be from Avril, but Mr Gough now argued that it could have been deposited at any time since the pillowcases had last been changed, some three weeks before Avril had died. This, together with the discrepancy in what Ian Baker had said, led Deemster Cain to rule that the prisoner should plead again once the jury had been brought back into court.

When asked to make that plea, Frank Griffin said that he was not guilty to murder, but would plead guilty to manslaughter. The prosecution accepted that defence and, on the deemster's instructions, the jury were ordered to return a formal not guilty verdict to the charge of murder. Sentencing was then deferred to 1 September.

On 1 September, Griffin was back in court to hear that sentence. Before judgement was given, the defence produced character witnesses' statements, including two from Avril's daughters, explaining that Frank was a kind and dutiful husband and asking for leniency. Deemster William Cain then sentenced Griffin to two years' imprisonment, adding, 'What you did to your wife was extremely dangerous, even though you had no intent to kill her or do her severe bodily harm.'

19

The Best of Friends

Bernard Aitken and Graham Joseph Murphy had been close friends in Scotland, but in the early 1990s Murphy's family moved to the Isle of Man and the two men obviously saw little of each other; but then, in 1997, Aitken too travelled to the island and found employment for himself. The friendship was rekindled and the two were often out drinking together.

Unfortunately, that was a problem. It was true that when the two were sober, they were indeed the very best of friends, but once either or both of them had had a drink, they became argumentative and quarrelsome and even fought each other. One such incident took place in the autumn of 1997 when both men were arrested after an incident in Mona Street, Douglas. Both men sustained injuries in the fight and both refused to make complaints against each other to the police. As a result, in September of that year, they were both bound over to keep the peace.

By June 1998, Aitken was twenty-three and his friend Murphy was eighteen. On Saturday, 20 June, both men went out drinking, but this time they were not together. Aitken, who lived in Kingswood Grove, spent that afternoon drinking lager and vodka in the houses of some other friends in Pulrose and also at the Pinewood Hotel. Murphy, who lived in the Rent-a-Chalet complex in Victoria Road, Douglas, ended up that evening at his girlfriend's home in Hazel Crescent.

Michele McBurnie, the mother of Murphy's two-year-old son Stephen, found him to be in a rather argumentative mood and obviously, in her opinion, very drunk, so at one stage she asked him to leave the house. Meanwhile, at about the same time, Aitken arrived at the house of David Murphy, Graham's brother, in Laburnum Road, Pulrose.

David Murphy shared the house with Katie Campbell and her two daughters. She too thought that her visitor was in a rather strange mood and suffering from the effects of alcohol but, rather than asking him to leave, she decided to take her children to a neighbour's house. Katie took one of the girls with her at first, and asked if she could stay until Aitken decided to leave. The neighbour agreed that Katie could do so and she then returned to her home to collect her second daughter, and to finally tell Aitken that she wanted him to leave. On the way there she met Graham Murphy, told him that Aitken was at her house, and that she wanted him to leave. Murphy said he would accompany her there and make sure that Aitken left.

When Katie and Murphy arrived at the house at 39 Laburnum Road, Aitken refused to let them in at first. Eventually he relented and opened the door and immediately an argument broke out between the two men. Katie asked them both to leave, but they ignored her request – and then Murphy escalated matters by punching Aitken in the face.

It was at this point that Aitken picked up a steak knife and brandished it towards Murphy. Murphy glanced down at the weapon and said, 'Are we going to start playing like that, are we?' Aitken did not reply, but lunged forward once and stabbed Murphy in his chest. As Murphy fell backwards, Katie Campbell ran screaming from the house with her daughter and was soon telephoning for an ambulance.

When the paramedics arrived, at 7.10 p.m., they found Aitken cradling the injured man in his arms. Despite prompt medical attention, nothing could be done for Murphy and he was pronounced dead at the scene. A deeply remorseful Aitken was taken into custody and duly charged with murder.

Perhaps it said much for the area where the crime took place that, even as the police and paramedics were attending, a crowd of fifty to sixty people gathered around the Laburnum Road area. Some of them had also been drinking, and in fact two had to be arrested by the police for public order offences.

At the various court hearings it was revealed that the dead man had worked for Krypton Cleaning Services. He had been born in East Kilbride and had moved to the island with his family which included two brothers and a sister. His mother, Christine Marshall, was quoted as saying, 'He was just a brilliant boy who was loved very much by all his family and friends.'

Dr Edmund Thorp, a Home Office pathologist who had flown over to the island on the day after the stabbing, Sunday, 21 June, reported that the single stab wound was the cause of death. Other witnesses were called who said that, soon after the attack, Aitken had been seen putting the knife down a drain in Pulrose Road but he had then returned to the house in Laburnum Road and cradled the injured man in his arms. The knife had later been recovered by the police and shown to be the weapon responsible for Graham Murphy's death.

Bernard Aitken finally faced his trial in November 1999, before Deemster Kerruish. Aitken was defended by Mr Terence McDonald, while the case for the prosecution lay in the hands of Mr Alastair Montgomerie. The accused man pleaded not guilty to murder, but guilty to manslaughter – a plea that was accepted by the prosecution. Sentence was, however, deferred pending a social inquiry report.

On Thursday, 2 December 1999, the court assembled again for sentencing. Here it was shown that Aitken had come from a dysfunctional family. He was estranged from his mother, and his father had been an alcoholic who beat him. Aitken also had previous convictions including one for assault and others for burglary. Furthermore, the social inquiry report stated that unless he received some form of professional help, there was a likelihood that he would commit violent crime again. However, he had also shown genuine remorse for what he had done and apparently had little recollection of the event itself.

Sentencing him to six and a half years for manslaughter, Deemster Kerruish added, 'You will carry the guilt of your actions for the rest of your life.'

In due course, Bernard Aitken was taken off the island and sent to serve his sentence in his native Scotland. In March 2002, it was announced that he was due for release from Shotts Prison in Lanarkshire, having served some two and a half years. At the time, Christine Marshall, whose son had been killed, expressed an interest in meeting Aitken, and he had agreed to this but the process had been blocked by the authorities.

Christine had said that she wanted to see Aitken so that she could understand precisely what happened and why. She wanted to know if her son's killer felt remorse for what he had done, and for him to know how it had affected her family. The authorities, in the form of the mediation service SACRO, were not to be moved and advised the prison against it.

20

A Duty of Care

At 8.25 p.m. on Tuesday, 13 July 1999, 79-year-old Marion Ethel Dennis was admitted to Noble's Hospital in Douglas. She had been transferred from the Ballastowell Garden Nursing Home in Ramsey, suffering from terrible bedsores. Despite excellent medical treatment, including an operation to relieve her suffering, Marion died exactly one week later, on Tuesday, 20 July 1999.

The hospital staff were far from happy with the care Marion had apparently been receiving in the Ramsey nursing home and involved the police in an investigation into her death. That in turn led to two arrests and, in due course, the nursing home manager, Dennis Anthony Latham, and his deputy, Barbara Jean Campbell, found themselves facing a charge of manslaughter.

Latham, thirty-four, had taken over as manager of the home in February 1998. Campbell, sixty-two, had taken over as assistant or deputy manager later that same year, in August, and was a qualified nurse. The trial of the two accused opened on Tuesday, 21 September 2003, before acting Deemster Rowe, the prosecution case being led by Mr Michael Shorrock who was assisted by Ms Linda Watts. Campbell's defence lay in the hands of Mr Brian Higgs, assisted by Mr Jerry Carter, while Latham was defended by Mr David Aubrey and Mr Darren Taubitz.

Medical evidence would prove to be of critical importance in this case. Among the many witnesses was Dr Hilary Clarke who had been called to the nursing home on 13 January 1999.

She told the court that she had been surprised at the severity of Marion's bedsores and it had been her who referred Marion to Noble's Hospital.

Mary Noble was a surgical ward manager at the hospital and she had had care of Marion from the morning after her admission, Wednesday, 14 July. She reported a horrendous and offensive smell, like rotting flesh. In fact, the odour, which was coming from the unfortunate woman's bed, was so bad that she had to be moved to a different ward.

Questioned further by Mr Shorrock, Mary Noble said that she had seen two large pressure sores on each of the lower buttocks of her patient. She had not seen sores of such severity since her student days in 1969 since which time the treatment of such cases had improved a thousandfold. Mary Noble was also able to testify that Marion had been very thin and appeared to be malnourished, and that part of her treatment was to get as much food as possible inside her. To illustrate the severity of this malnourishment, Mary pointed out that the level of plasma protein in Marion's blood had shown a reading of 20, when the average level of a healthy person was between 36 and 52.

Dr Martin Barcos was working as a locum house officer at Noble's Hospital during Marion's stay. He stated that the pressure sores she suffered from were a significant contributory factor in her death. Marion had undergone an operation to relieve the sores, on 18 July, but had died two days later.

Dr Georgina Cassie was a surgical house officer at Noble's and described the two bedsores as being about the size of her clenched fist. She had never before seen pressure sores that severe.

Dr William Lawler, a consultant Home Office pathologist, had performed the postmortem on Marion Dennis, on 24 July, four days after she had died. He reported a skin deficit of some 9 by 5 centimetres on the right lower buttock, which extended deep into the tissue. There was also a skin deficit some 7 by 5 centimetres on the left lower buttock. In Dr Lawler's opinion, these wounds had led to renal failure and septicaemia with the actual cause of death being bronchopneumonia. The heavily infected tissues had contributed significantly to Marion's death, and the other factors would not have occurred when they did had she not suffered from those ulcers.

Some of the history of Marion Dennis was then given. Marion had been a former shop proprietor and had come to the island with her husband John after they had retired. John lived in Kermode Close, Ramsey, but had died two months after Marion, in September 1999. The couple had had no children.

Marion had apparently suffered a long history of medical problems including hypertension. Part of her right lung had been removed in 1992 due to tuberculosis. She had suffered a severe stroke in 1994 and, as a result, her right side was completely paralysed and her speech was impaired. She was also incontinent.

On 29 November 1998, she had been admitted to the Ramsey Cottage Hospital. She had needed treatment for ulcers on her lower left leg while there, but these had been healing well by the time she was admitted to the Ballastowell Home on 1 March 1999. The staff there should have been fully aware of that medical history and the consequent likelihood of Marion developing fresh problems as far as bedsores and ulcers were concerned.

A medical report had been prepared by Professor Michael Horan, who was the professor of geriatric medicine at the University of Manchester. He described the care given to Marion at the nursing home as 'rather haphazard'. She had apparently spent long periods of time either sitting in a chair or sitting up in bed and this would have only served to make the situation worse and would actually impede any healing process. He also stated that, in his opinion, the sores had been eminently treatable.

Professor Horan was also asked about a de-sloughing procedure that Dennis Latham had carried out to ease the problem.

This had taken place on 29 June and Latham had used a stitch-cutter to perform the task. In Professor Horan's opinion, this instrument was not suitable for the purpose. The professor ended his report by saying, 'There is no doubt in my mind that this woman died directly as a result of her pressure ulcers. The management of the pressure ulcers was inadequate.'

Other medical evidence came from members of staff at the nursing home. Nicola Ball was employed by the Kennedy Nursing Agency and went to work at the home in July 1999. She only started work a day or two before Marion had been admitted to Noble's, but she recalled the pressure sores and also that, since Marion was incontinent, the dressings were frequently soiled. This meant that the various bodily fluids came into contact with the wounds.

In order to properly treat the wounds, Marion Dennis should have had the use of an air mattress. Nurse Kerry Coulter testified that there were only two such mattresses in the nursing home, and one of those belonged to a resident. That left one for the remainder of the residents. That mattress was being used by Dorothy Cooksey, another resident, but she died on 8 March. From 9 March, the day afterwards, the mattress was used by Marion Dennis.

Another nurse, Michael Yates, testified that there was no real care plan outlined for Marion Dennis. There were no notes about when she had last seen a doctor, so on 4 July he called out Dr Armour. The doctor examined her and looked at the dressings on the pressure sores, but said he thought she might have had a stroke. Yates was unable to say if the doctor had actually looked at the wounds beneath the dressings.

Michael Chevalier was another agency nurse at the home and he reported that Marion had been lying on a ripple mattress but it had not been plugged in. That meant that she was lying there without any pressure relief. Michael had spoken to Barbara Campbell about his concerns about the type of dressing used on Marion, but said Barbara did not seem to be interested.

John Appleyard was a nurse at the home and he said he had discussed Marion's wounds with Dennis Latham. According to Appleyard, Latham had said that the wounds were clean and were being managed with treatment. Appleyard had also spoken to Barbara Campbell and suggested that a doctor be brought in to examine Marion. Barbara had replied, 'Doctors are not the experts, the nurses are the experts. We should tell them what to prescribe.' On 8 March, Appleyard had made a written record that there was no pressure relief device on Marion's bed.

Dennis Latham did step into the witness box to give his own testimony. Referring to Barbara Campbell, Latham stated that he had had complete trust in her. She had come to him with excellent references and was a registered nurse and a registered midwife. He agreed, however, that as the manager of the nursing home team, the final responsibility for patient care rested with him.

The trial lasted for a total of five weeks. In his summing up for the prosecution, Michael Shorrock stated that, when she had left the Ramsey Cottage Hospital, Marion had only a small sore which had been left uncovered and her medical history meant that she was a prime candidate for pressure sores. He went on to quote from a brochure advertising the services at Ballastowell which stated, among other things, that patients would receive '... the highest standard of care, provided by staff who had all the skills and experience necessary in the specialist care of the elderly'.

The verdict, when it finally came, was that both defendants were guilty as charged. Sentencing was postponed to 1 December and, on that date, Dennis Latham received a sentence of two and a half years while Barbara Campbell was given one year. She did not appeal against her sentence, but in January 2004 Latham did and succeeded in having his sentence reduced by six months.

The final episode in this tragic case took place in July 2006. In that month, the Nursing and Midwifery Council concluded its own investigation into what had taken place at Ballastowell. The result of that inquiry was that both Latham and Campbell were formally struck off. William Buxton, the chairman, said in his summing up, 'It is difficult to conceive of a more serious breach of a nurse's duty than a lack of care which results in a patient's death. They were responsible for the care of the residents and failed to provide such care under the professional code. Their care fell so far short it resulted in her premature death.'

21

Other Crimes Post-1900

Many of the crimes committed after 1900 are covered in separate chapters within this book. The following additional cases took place from 1900 onwards.

Thomas and William Corlett – 1900

William Corlett and his father, Thomas, ran a butcher's shop from Bucks Road in Douglas. By all accounts, the shop was a very busy one and William liked to unwind sometimes by enjoying a relaxing game of billiards.

On Monday, 7 May 1900, William was in a billiards hall in Regent Street, and saw two men he knew well, Herbert Cowell and John Davies, playing at one of the tables. Kindly, William offered to score for them, but some way into the game Cowell accused him of scoring incorrectly, to the favour of his opponent. An argument broke out and this developed into a scuffle during which Corlett struck Cowell in the face.

This altercation was seen by the club manager, James Roberts, who came over to stop the fight. Matters ended with both Corlett and Cowell being thrown out into the street. By now, it was around 1 a.m. on Tuesday, 8 May.

At 9.20 a.m. on that same Tuesday, Cowell was drinking in the bar at the Villiers Hotel, where the barman, Thomas Hales, asked him about the fresh bruise he was now sporting on his cheek. Cowell told him the story of the fight with William Corlett and implied that he was going off to sort things out

Loch Promenade, Douglas. To the far left is the Villiers Hotel where Herbert Cowell had a drink before going to face Thomas and William Corlett

once and for all. Hales saw him leave the bar and drive off in his pony and trap.

William Corlett wasn't in the shop at the time Cowell pulled up outside, but his father was. After some minutes, Thomas went outside to ask Cowell what he wanted and heard him say that he had come to give William a thrashing. Thomas, of course, knew about the incident at the billiards hall and told Cowell that he ought to be careful and leave matters as they were in case he found himself on the wrong end of another beating. Cowell took exception to these remarks and drove his trap off up the street. He was back after a few minutes, though, and at about the same time William Corlett arrived back at the shop, on his bicycle.

William parked his bicycle and Cowell tied up his pony and the two men then met in the middle of the street. Cowell was seen to push Corlett away, whereupon Corlett removed his coat and took a swing at his opponent. The punch connected and Cowell fell to the ground.

Cowell was soon on his feet and at this Thomas cried out for his son to 'Give him another' which William Corlett duly did. This second punch knocked Cowell backwards and he fell, striking his head on the kerb. It was clear that he was now very badly hurt indeed.

William and Thomas Corlett lifted the unconscious Cowell on to his own trap and drove him to the hospital. While the injured man was being attended to, William walked to the police station and gave his version of what had taken place, pointing out that this had been a fair fist fight and there had been no intention to hurt Cowell. He was allowed to leave but, after Cowell died at 10 p.m., William Cowell was duly arrested.

The inquest opened before the coroner, Mr Samuel Harris, and here it became plain that perhaps this hadn't been a fair fist fight after all. There had been various witnesses in the street who could confirm some of the story given by William and Thomas, but others had seen Thomas actually help Cowell to his feet after that first blow, before encouraging his son to hit him again.

Dr John Alfred Deardon had carried out the postmortem and he had found a large blood clot around Cowell's brain, together with a fractured skull. The wound on the back of his head was consistent with Cowell striking the kerb and he had died as a result of pressure to his brain.

Now that evidence had been heard which gave Thomas Corlett a greater degree of involvement in the attack, he found himself arrested on Friday, 11 May. Originally, both men were then charged with murder, but after the evidence had all been detailed, on Saturday, 12 May, it was decided to send both of them for trial on the lesser charge of manslaughter.

The trial of the two Corletts opened in November and, after all the witnesses had given their evidence again, the jury retired to consider their verdicts. Both men were found guilty, after a deliberation of some twenty minutes, but the jury did recommend mercy as far as the sentencing was concerned.

It seemed that this recommendation did have an effect for William Corlett, who had struck Cowell that fatal blow, was sentenced to just six months' imprisonment, with hard labour. His father, Thomas, who had encouraged William to strike a second blow, received three months, again with hard labour.

John Pearson – 1910

In the year 1908, John Pearson and his wife left England and took up residence at the Crown Hotel in Parliament Street, Ramsey. For the most part, Pearson was a capable landlord but there was one problem. He had a violent temper and was easily roused to anger, especially in drink, and as a consequence, made more than one appearance in court.

There were two domestic servants working at the hotel – Ellen Jane Loughlin and Ethel Mary Walker – and there seemed to be something of an atmosphere between Pearson and Ellen Loughlin. No one could say with certainty what the problem was, but there was certainly something. Pearson was constantly finding fault with her work, but Ellen could give as good as she got and often answered her employer back.

Things seemed to come to a head in early August 1910, when Ellen announced that she was looking for a new position. Indeed, she actually left the Crown for a few days, but Pearson begged her to return – which she did. It did not improve the atmosphere, though, and things went on much as before.

On Sunday, 14 August 1910, Pearson's wife, Jane, went to morning church with a friend of hers, Mary Ellen Brain. It was now around 11 a.m. and only Pearson and the two servants were left inside the public house.

John Pearson was a creature of habit and it was his custom, each day, to go to a nearby barber's shop run by George Whewell, in order to get a shave. At around 11.20 a.m., Pearson walked the few yards from the Crown to Whewell's shop, only to find that there was a large queue of men waiting to be served. Pearson said he would call back, but when he did – some ten minutes later – there was still quite a long queue. Rather than wait any longer, Pearson asked Whewell if he would call at the Crown at about 1 p.m. and shave him then. Whewell agreed, but it was an appointment he would never keep.

It was close on 11.30 a.m. when Ethel Walker heard two rapid shots come from the backyard of the Crown. Looking out of the back window, she saw Ellen Loughlin lying on the ground. This was followed almost immediately by the sound of Pearson running upstairs. Another shot rang out and Ethel ran outside to get some assistance.

Three policemen were soon in attendance. Inspector Quilliam, together with Constables Callister and Gowne, entered the Crown and began to look for Pearson. Bravely, knowing that his man was almost certainly armed, Inspector Quilliam went upstairs in time to see Pearson dashing from one room into another. Quilliam duly took his man into custody, but it was plain that medical attention was the most important factor at this stage – for half of Pearson's face had been blown away.

John Pearson still exhibited violent tendencies even though he was badly injured. He resisted attempts to take him to the Ramsey Cottage Hospital but, finally, was attended to at that establishment. It was all to no avail and Pearson died at 2 p.m. that same day.

Two separate inquests were held the next day, before the coroner, Mr J. M. Cruickshank. First, inquiries were made into the death of Pearson. The various witnesses to the strained relationship between Pearson and Ellen were heard and then Dr W. S. Cowan gave details of the injuries the dead man had suffered.

In Dr Cowan's opinion, the wound could only be explained by assuming that Pearson had placed the double-barrelled shotgun found at the scene underneath his chin and fired upwards. The blood loss sustained had claimed Pearson's life and the jury found no difficulty in deciding that Pearson had taken his own life while of unsound mind.

The proceedings now turned to the death of Ellen Loughlin. Again Dr Cowan was called to give evidence, saying that she had suffered two wounds. One, to the back of her neck, had snapped her spinal column and death would have been instantaneous. The second wound was to Ellen's right upper arm. Both were gunshot wounds and the weapon had been held close to her when it was fired. Once again the jury had little trouble with the evidence and duly returned a verdict that Ellen had been killed by John Pearson.

The day after the inquests had concluded, Tuesday, 16 August, John Pearson was laid to rest. The following day, Wednesday, 17 August, Ellen Loughlin's body was also buried. No one could ever state, with certainty, why such a terrible crime had ever taken place.

John Williams – 1916

In 1914, the war to end all wars broke out across a divided Europe. Very soon after hostilities had begun, it was realized that the Allies would take a goodly number of prisoners and somewhere had to be found to keep them. What better place than a small island in the middle of the Irish Sea? So, a large camp was set up in Douglas to take some of these prisoners.

The bloody war dragged on and the number of prisoners increased so a second camp was set up near Peel. It was known as Knockaloe and it was there that Sergeant John Williams, originally from Warrington, was assigned. Another one of the Allied servicemen at that camp was Colour Sergeant William Henry Malings and, coincidentally, he too came from Warrington, though there is no evidence that the two knew each other before arriving at Knockaloe.

At noon on 15 May 1916, there were four men in the sergeants' mess at the camp. In addition to Malings and Williams, there was also Lance Sergeant James Slingsby Clare and Sergeant Major Stringfellow. The four men enjoyed a beer and then had lunch. After their meal all four sat together talking and the atmosphere between them was perfectly normal and friendly.

Not long after the four had eaten they were joined by Sergeant Frederick William Stoll. There were now five men in the mess hut but, at around 2.50 p.m., Williams left, saying that he was going to use the toilet. Very soon after this, Malings left, saying that he would return shortly. A few minutes later, Stringfellow left so that now only Stoll and Clare were left inside the mess.

Private Brown was outside the sergeant's mess and saw Malings leave. The sergeant was easily recognizable since he had some sort of back problem that necessitated him walking with the aid of a stick. Brown saw the sergeant walking towards his own hut in the company of Corporal Unsworth. The two men parted and Malings went into his billet. Almost immediately, a single shot rang out.

Corporal Unsworth was the first man inside the hut. He found Sergeant Malings lying on the floor, not far from the doorway, with blood issuing from his neck. The only other occupant of the room was Sergeant Williams who was standing at the other side of the hut.

Malings was already dead and it appeared that the man who had shot him must be Williams. The police were called and Williams duly taken into custody to face a charge of wilful murder.

The inquest on the dead man opened the following day but only evidence of identification was given, by Captain Henry Cosby-Stokes. Matters were then adjourned to 22 May.

When the inquest proceedings reconvened, medical evidence was given by Dr Robert McGeah who had performed the postmortem. He reported a wound in the top of Malings's chest with a corresponding exit wound on his back. There was no mark of scorching or burning so the bullet must have been fired from some distance. In Dr McGeah's opinion, death would have been instantaneous.

The jury had no difficulty in returning a verdict of murder

against Williams and his trial for that crime opened on Tuesday, 8 August, before Deemster Moore. The attorney-general, Mr G. A. Ring, outlined the case for the prosecution while Williams was defended by Mr H. P. Kelly.

Though there had been no known antagonism between Malings and Williams, evidence was now given of the prisoner's rather strange behaviour after the shooting. Sergeant Harrison had heard Williams say, 'The cur has been the cause of all my troubles and I have made a clean job of it.' Another witness, Corporal Phillips, had heard him announce, 'I am rid of that bastard. I am satisfied.' There was also the fact that even while the body was being examined at the scene, and the room searched, Williams had calmly read a newspaper and smoked his pipe.

In his summing up, Deemster Moore told the jury that this could not be a case of manslaughter. There was no question of the shooting being accidental so the only two verdicts open to them were guilty of murder or guilty while suffering from mental incapacity.

The jury were out for less than twenty minutes and returned to say that they had found Williams guilty of murder, but that he was of unsound mind at the time he committed the crime. Williams was then ordered to be confined during His Majesty's Pleasure. No motive for the shooting of Sergeant Malings was ever discovered.

Karlo Albin Salminen – 1943

In some ways, the story of Karlo Salminen mirrors the previous entry as it also took place inside an internment camp.

During the Second World War a number of such camps were again set up on the Isle of Man, including ones at Peel, Douglas, Port Erin and Ramsey. It is this latter camp, the Mooragh at Ramsey, that is involved in this story.

Most readers may assume that the only prisoners taken by the Allies, in Europe, between 1939 and 1945 were either

German or Italian. What is perhaps less well known is that Finland also fought on the Axis side, but matters were not as clear cut as that. Some Finns were totally anti-Russian and therefore pro-German, but many others felt the opposite way and supported the Russians and therefore the rest of the Allies. This led to internal conflicts and great tensions within the Finnish area of the Mooragh camp.

Karlo Salminen had been born in the United States and worked as a sailor in the Finnish Merchant Navy. He was pro-Allies and duly registered as an alien when he arrived on board a ship that docked at Liverpool in 1941. However, when he returned to that city in the October of the same year, he failed to rejoin his ship at the correct time so found himself arrested and finally sent to the Mooragh camp in December 1941.

Nestor Huppunen was also Finnish, but he was pro-German. He had been born in Finland and, like Salminen, worked as a seaman. When he arrived in Britain he was arrested and found himself sent to the internment camp at Douglas in May 1942. Later that same year, in November, he was sent on to the camp at Ramsey where Salminen had already been for almost a full year.

At this time there were about 400 Finns in their part of the Mooragh camp and most were pro-Russian. These individuals found themselves trusted rather more than the pro-German faction and, as a result, were allowed out of the camp to work on the land. Further, some of them were then sent to other camps in mainland Britain. This process had two effects. First, it caused even greater antagonism between the pro-German faction and those who supported the Allies, but perhaps more importantly, since those who supported the Allies were often sent back to England, it inexorably altered the balance within the camp. Slowly, the group of Finns as a whole became more and more pro-German until, by April 1943, they finally outnumbered their countrymen who supported the Allies by a factor of almost three to one.

There were also other problems inside the Finnish camp,

including one with alcohol usage. Many of the inmates made their own illegal alcohol from anything they could find, but on Sunday, 18 April 1943, the beer store was raided and the entire contents stolen. That night there was, as a result, a great deal of rowdy behaviour, fuelled by drink, and many pro-Allies prisoners were beaten up by their countrymen. The atmosphere inside the camp was growing steadily more and more strained.

Two days after this, on Tuesday, 20 April, Karlo Salminen asked permision to go outside the camp. In order to do so he dressed himself in his best suit, a clear sign that he was not only about to go outside, but also that he was therefore a supporter of the Allies.

At around 12.10 p.m., Huppunen was cleaning out Hut 9 when he came to the door, carrying a bucket filled with dirty water. At that precise moment, Salminen was walking past the hut, dressed in his suit. Huppunen immediately threw the water over Salminen, causing a scuffle to break out between the two men. It was during that scuffle that Salminen reached into his pocket, took out a knife, and stabbed Huppunen. As the injured man fell to the ground, others who had seen the attack surrounded Salminen and it was clear that he was about to receive a severe beating at the hands of the pro-German Finns.

The entire attack had been witnessed by an inmate of the German camp next door. Martin Scholtz was a doctor and he knew that Huppunen, and possibly Salminen himself by now, would be in need of urgent medical attention. Scholtz ran to the camp hospital and told Dr Templeton what he had just seen. The two medics then went to the Finnish camp to find Salminen being beaten by his fellow prisoners and Huppunen lying on the ground, already dead.

Salminen was rescued from his attackers and taken to Noble's Hospital in Douglas. His injuries necessitated a stay of several weeks in hospital, and it was not until 13 May that he was discharged – only to be immediately arrested and charged with murder.

Salminen's trial opened on 15 June before Deemster Cowley. The Attorney-General, Mr Ramsey Bignall Moore, outlined the case for the prosecution while Salminen was defended by Mr R. K. Eason. Much of the evidence was given in camera and the proceedings would last until 19 June.

Various witnesses were called who had seen the attack upon Huppunen and medical testimony was given by Dr John McAlister who had performed the postmortem. He reported a single wound, some three-quarters of an inch long, which lay between the fifth and sixth ribs on the right-hand side. Death was due to haemorrhage.

For his own part, Salminen admitted that he had stabbed Huppunen but claimed that he had only meant to frighten him. As for the weapon, this was a table knife that he had taken and sharpened by rubbing it on some cement.

The jury took seventy-five minutes to decide upon their verdict and, when it came, it was that not only was Salminen not guilty of murder but, rather surprisingly perhaps, he was not guilty of manslaughter either. The prisoner was then discharged and returned to the camp at Ramsey. He only remained there for a few more days, however, and on 21 June he was shipped off the island to a camp in England.

The Murder of Marjorie Ashton – 1995

On 1 May 1995, the body of 72-year-old pensioner Marjorie Ashton was found in her bungalow, Ingle Nook, at 41 Fuchsia Grove on the Silverburn Estate at Ballasalla. She had been strangled. Despite pleas for assistance from the public, no one could be found who could shed any light on the murder and it remained, for some considerable time, one of the few unsolved murders on the island. There were, however, other events on the Isle of Man that were never satisfactorily explained.

There was, for example, the tragic death of Dorothy Harris, who also lived in Ballasalla, at Glashen Terrace. She died in a house fire in February 1996, and although this was said to be an accident, her brother, Ted Halsall, who lived in Wigan, was never convinced. He believed that there had been a break-in and that the fire had been started afterwards by the burglar, probably to destroy any evidence. Unfortunately, there simply wasn't enough evidence left to proceed and a verdict of accidental death was returned at the subsequent inquest.

There were other mysteries too. Before these two ladies had died, a 32-year-old Onchan man, Laurence James Thomas Smith, had simply disappeared. On Saturday, 9 April 1994, his red Ford Escort was found in a car park near the bus station in Douglas. He was never seen again but, as he was known to be suffering from depression, enquiries into his disappearance were never particularly thorough.

In the same month that Dorothy Harris died in the house fire, a man named Kenneth Robert Fletcher had also disappeared. Fletch, as he was known, lived in Minorca Hill, Laxey, and was aged just twenty-eight when he vanished on 12 February 1996. He was never seen again.

At the time, there was no suggestion that any of these events might be connected in any way.

Two years after this, in October 1998, a house fire in Blackpool claimed the life of 75-year-old Jemima Cargill. The following month, also in Blackpool, a double murder shocked the resort. Joan Boardman, aged seventy-four, was strangled at her home at Seafield Road. Her body was then placed in such a way that when her husband, Eric, saw it, he would go into the room where her killer was waiting for him – the result being that Eric was then battered to death. The killer had, however, left behind the cosh he had used, together with his fingerprints. It was those prints that led to the arrest of Stephen Akinmurele, a man with a string of previous convictions for burglary and assaults, especially on the elderly. His criminal record went back to 1989, when he was just eleven years old.

Stephen was born in Nigeria in 1978 where he lived until the age of seven. He was then sent to the Isle of Man to live with his grandmother, first at Castletown and then later at Douglas. In 1996 he had moved to Blackpool where he obtained employment as a civil servant working at the local job centre. At night he had a second job as a barman, and it soon became clear that he had lodged with Jemima Cargill who had died in the house fire. It wasn't long before Akinmurele found himself charged with three murders, those of Jemima Cargill and both of the Boardmans. Matters though, did not end there.

Further investigations led to Akinmurele admitting his part in other murders, including those of Marjorie Ashton and Dorothy Harris on the Isle of Man. He was duly charged with those crimes but also admitted killing a rambler on the island and burying his body on a cliff overlooking the sea. Police on the island were informed, but a search of the area found nothing. He was also suspected of being involved in the disappearance of Kenneth Fletcher.

Akinmurele was held on remand at Manchester prison, but it was clear that he was a danger not only to others but also to himself. In August 1999 he tried to kill himself by taking an overdose of medication he had been prescribed. Held in the hospital wing, he was found to have a sharpened toothbrush and admitted that he had thought of attacking and killing a female member of staff.

Various court appearances followed and in due course it was decided that although he had been charged with two murders on the Isle of Man, those charges could not be proceeded with. It was held that a British court had no jurisdiction over crimes committed on the island. No doubt the authorities would advise a second trial on those charges once the Blackpool cases had been dealt with.

Akinmurele's trial was due to begin at Preston on 27 September 1999, but events would rule that the proceedings never took place. On the afternoon of Saturday, 28 August, Akinmurele tore some strips of material from items of his clothing, tied them to the window in his cell, and hanged himself. He was found by prison staff who gave him the kiss of life but without success.

At the subsequent inquest, a note left behind by Akinmurele was read out. Addressed to his mother it read, 'I couldn't take any more of feeling like how I do now, always wanting to kill.' The murder of Marjorie Ashton was no longer marked as unsolved.

Andrew George Dickson – 2000

Keith Kirby was something of a loner. A married man, estranged from his wife, Maureen, he now lived alone in Hutchinson Square, Douglas. He was, however, still close to his family, especially his two children – Kevin, twelve, and Lyndsey, nine.

A creature of habit, Keith saw his children every weekend. He liked nothing more than to have them stay over with him on Saturday night and to watch his son play football. As for Lyndsey, when she pleaded for a hamster, Keith bought her one which he kept at his flat because his wife was frightened of the animal. Lyndsey was delighted and called her new pet Holly. She was so excited that she even stayed with her father for an extra night, on Sunday, even though it was school the next day.

For the most part, Keith Kirby kept himself to himself. He liked to go out drinking and one of his favourite haunts was Studebaker's club. Things were just the same on Thursday, 27 January 2000. Alone, Keith went to Studebaker's at some time before midnight and had a few quiet drinks. The club wasn't very busy that night, with perhaps just forty or fifty patrons, and no one really noticed as Keith left later – at 1.45 a.m. – in the company of two men.

It was a man walking home who found Keith Kirby's body in an alleyway off Mona Drive, between the Ravenswood flats and the Mereside Hotel, at a few minutes after 2.00 a.m. on Friday, 28 January. He had been badly beaten about the head and was pronounced dead at the scene. The police were now looking for a murderer.

As part of the early investigations, officers spoke to a number of Keith's friends. One recalled an incident some four days before Keith had been killed. This friend had been walking down Somerset Road at 3.30 p.m. on Monday, 24 January, and had seen Keith in an apparent argument with two young men. They seemed to be threatening him and the friend was able to give police descriptions of both men. One was white, around 6 feet 3 inches tall, skinny, with short cropped hair. Perhaps his most distinctive feature was that he had a rather flattened nose, similar to that displayed by some boxers. His companion was also white, shorter at 5 feet 7 inches, and with dark hair, which curled close to his collar.

Other lines of enquiry were also followed up. For example, there had been a disturbance outside the Carousel Café which was situated next to the Imperial Hotel, at the bottom of Mona Drive. This had involved a number of young men and had taken place at 1.30 a.m. Another disturbance had taken place in Mona Drive itself, just before the discovery of Keith's body. Finally, police were anxious to trace a man and a woman who had been picked up in a taxi outside Toffs nightclub at 1.57 a.m. and taken to Glen Vine.

The most promising lead, though, came from the closed-circuit cameras outside Studebaker's. Many of the patrons seen there that night were soon traced by the police, or came forward to give statements of their own accord. Two men, however, did not come forward and hadn't yet been traced. They had been recorded as entering the club at 11.44 p.m. on the Thursday and pictures of these two men, taken from the camera, were published in the newspapers – leading to their arrests.

Andrew George Dickson was twenty-nine and lived in Conister Road, Willaston. His brother, Mark, was younger, twenty-five, and lived in Belmont Terrace. Both men were interviewed at length and this led to Andrew being charged with murder and his brother Mark facing two charges of assisting Andrew in avoiding arrest.

There were various court appearances during which more background was given on Keith Kirby. He had been a production worker for a company named Strix, at Ronaldsway airport. Born on Merseyside, he had moved to the island as a young boy, with his parents, and had grown up and been educated there. He had married Maureen in 1977, but they had separated in 1998. His wife, a bank employee, had remained on friendly terms with Keith and had last seen him alive on Sunday, 23 January, when she went to his flat to see the hamster he had bought for his daughter.

Andrew Dickson finally appeared in court to answer the murder charge on Monday, 9 February 2001, before Deemster Kerruish. He was represented by Ms Louise Byrne and pleaded guilty. He explained that he had deliberately lured Keith from Studebaker's with the promise of some after-hours drinking. He had not intended to kill Keith, but then suddenly exploded and hit him. He then picked up a breeze block and used it to batter Keith to death, striking him about the head several times. Matters were then adjourned for reports, prior to sentencing.

Exactly one month later, on Monday, 9 March, Andrew Dickson was sentenced to life imprisonment with the recommendation that he should serve a minimum of fifteen years. As for his brother, Mark, he received a ten-month suspended prison sentence for helping Andrew evade arrest.

Anne Marie Gosling – 2004

Peter Roy Ormiston had been born in Ramsbottom, Lancashire, but spent most of his formative years in Whalley, near Clitheroe. He began his working life on the family farm run by his parents, Roy and Margaret, but eventually moved into the construction industry. Over the years he built up his own demolition company, based in Whalley, until in 2002 – at the age of forty-seven – he came to the Isle of Man.

It was a new start for Peter. He had been married, but the

relationship had ended and his two sons remained in Lancashire. Peter took a job as a driver for a construction company and in due course started a new relationship with a bank worker, Anne Marie Gosling. There was, however, one factor that spoiled this new start and that was that Anne suffered from psychiatric problems which were exacerbated when she drank alcohol.

Peter and Anne lived on the Clifton Park housing estate in Ramsey and for the most part were a happy enough couple. There were times when Anne's health problems became more of a concern, but most of the time they got on very well and had even discussed the possibility of getting married.

On Thursday, 22 January 2004, Anne rang the bank and said she felt too ill to go into work. The next day, Friday, 23 January, she also took off but felt she would be well enough to go back to work on the following Monday. That weekend she intended to spend with Peter and hoped that she would then feel much better for the new week.

On Sunday, 25 January, Anne and Peter were in a local pub, and though neither of them could be said to be drunk, it must be remembered that Anne's mental state was made worse by alcohol. They returned to their home at Magnus Court, King's Reach, some time before 4.30 p.m.

Anne would later claim that she had no memory of what had happened next. It seems as if there was some sort of argument or discussion, which ended with Peter saying he was going out for a walk. Anne took a knife from the kitchen, followed him outside, and stabbed him. She then returned to her flat and locked herself in, leaving Peter staggering towards a grass verge in Alkest Way. Peter's bleeding body was found by a passer-by who telephoned the emergency services. It was no use; Peter died just as the ambulance arrived.

It wasn't long before the police were knocking on the door of Anne's flat in Magnus Court. There was no reply and it appeared that Anne had barricaded herself in. Hostage negotiators were called and eventually entry was gained to the premises and Anne was taken into custody. That same evening, Dr Dick Shepherd performed the postmortem on Peter Ormiston.

Anne made her first appearance in court on Tuesday, 27 January, before the High Bailiff, Mr Michael Moyle. Evidence of arrest was given and the proceedings were adjourned until 10 February.

Various other hearings took place and it was not until Monday, 16 December 2004, that the evidence began to be outlined at the Court of General Gaol Delivery, before Deemster Doyle. This was merely a preliminary hearing to see what charge should be proceeded with at the subsequent trial. For the defence, Ms Dawn Jones suggested that a period of fourteen days would be needed for the trial.

Eventually, the trial was set for 19 September 2005, and Anne Gosling would be facing a charge of murder. In fact, delays put that trial date back and it then wasn't due to start until May 2006. However, before that, in late April, Anne said she wished to pleaded not guilty to murder but guilty to manslaughter, a plea accepted by Mr Stuart Neale for the prosecution.

Anne was taken back to court and appeared before acting Deemster Simon Fawcus. Some evidence was still heard. Dr Shepherd testified that Peter Ormiston had been stabbed three times with a kitchen knife, and bled to death.

A psychiatric report had been prepared by Aideen O'Halloran who highlighted a number of episodes of depression and anxiety suffered by Anne. There was also confirmation that drink had been a problem factor in her life for at least the previous fifteen years. Indeed, Anne had seen her GP a few months before the incident and his report showed that she was clearly depressed at the time.

The plea having been accepted, Anne was sentenced to serve a term of four and a half years in prison. However, since she had been held in custody since Peter's death, much of that time had already been served. Peter's family had travelled over to the island, hoping to see Anne jailed for life for murder and expressed their disgust at the leniency of the prison term. Peter's sister, Margaret Howard, said, 'As a family we have lost a son, a brother, a brother-in-law and an uncle, but most importantly, Peter's two sons have lost their dad. We were hoping for at least twenty years, but this sentence means she could be out in January.'

Lionel Barry Diamond – 2004

Paul Speller, who worked for Isle of Man Newspapers, had enjoyed a night out with friends and now, at around 12.30 a.m. on Saturday, 13 March 2004, he was walking to his home in Demesne Road, Douglas.

Suddenly, Paul heard the sound of breaking glass and assumed that it was some vandals causing problems after having drunk too much. However, just as he turned into Demesne Road itself he saw that there was a fire on the second floor of the building at the end of the row, number 44. The sight took Paul by surprise, not just because of the fire itself, but also because there was no alarm going off. The building was divided into flats and it was natural to assume that such an establishment should have some sort of alarm system fitted. Paul wasted no time in dialling 999 and calling out the emergency services.

In fact, other emergency calls had already been made by members of the public and, as a result, the fire service was on the scene within minutes of Paul's own call. Firemen wearing breathing apparatus moved into the building and began bringing people out, with the first person rescued being a small baby. Two men were then brought out, one being the father of the baby. Both men were attended by paramedics who used resuscitation equipment on them. In the case of the baby's father, this was successful, but he was still taken to Noble's Hospital in an ambulance. For the other man, 46-year-old Mark Laurence Doyle, the rescue attempts had come too late and he was pronounced dead on arrival at that same hospital.

44 Demesne Road, where a fire claimed the life of Mark Doyle in 2006

Mark Doyle was a native of Merseyside, living in West Kirby with his wife, Tracey, and two children: Olivia, seventeen, and Max, fifteen. An ambitious man, Mark had wanted to set up his own construction company and was working on the island to earn money to do that and to make a better life for his family. Usually he worked on the Isle of Man during the week and sometimes went home at weekends.

A popular man, Mark had been a rugby player before a broken leg had forced him into retirement and he was well known and well loved in his native city. Indeed, after his tragic death, Mike McCartney, the brother of Beatle Paul, and one of Mark's closest friends, told reporters, 'His birthday is around the same time as mine and we always shared parties. He was at my sixtieth recently and never have you seen someone so full of life. Mark was a lovely man and his family can be proud of him, and his children will have amazing memories of a marvellous man who was a great example of what a human being should be.'

Another tribute came from Pete Price, a Radio City DJ, who said, 'I think it is terrible a man can go off to work and never come back again. It's absolutely tragic. He was such a likeable man and his wife and children adored him.'

It soon became clear, though, that this tragedy was actually something that could have been avoided. Once the fire had been dampened down, fire officers began to investigate the cause and the circumstances.

The fire had started in Mark Doyle's second-floor flat – in the kitchen – but it was obvious that safety regulations had largely been ignored. There was no door to the kitchen, meaning that a fire starting there would be able to spread rapidly and without hindrance. The bedroom that Mark slept in did have a fire door, but this did not close properly. This meant that smoke from the kitchen fire spread easily throughout the flat and into Mark's bedroom. Indeed, a subsequent postmortem would show that smoke inhalation was the direct cause of death.

The conclusion was that fire safety regulations had not been followed and this negligence had led to the death of a man. The flats were owned by a company named Renaissance Enterprises Limited, and the issues raised by the fire led to charges against that company and the arrest of two officers of the company – Lionel Barry Diamond and Paula Judith Kermode. Eventually, the charges against Paula were dropped, but Lionel Diamond found himself facing a charge of manslaughter.

Diamond's trial for that offence opened in November 2006, before acting Deemster Simon Fawcus, and lasted for two weeks. At the end of that time, the seven-member jury found Diamond guilty of manslaughter and of five counts of breaching the Fire Precautions Flats Regulations of 1996. In addition, his company was found guilty of two charges of breaching those same regulations. Sentencing was then adjourned until Friday, 5 January 2007. Finally, on that Friday, Diamond was sentenced to fifteen months' imprisonment.

22

Full of Remorse

Leonard Thomas Osborne was the kind of man who would do a favour for anyone. In the past he had been an aircraft fitter but now, at the age of sixty-eight, he was a painter and decorator and lived with his wife, Shirley, in Keppel Road, Willaston.

In July 2000, Leonard was again doing someone a favour. His son had gone to Dublin and Leonard was looking after his cat. However, on the evening of Friday, 21 July, the cat had gone missing and Leonard had gone outside to look for it.

As Leonard walked down a lane behind Westbourne Drive, which ran from Ballakermeen Road to Hawarden Avenue, he spotted a young couple walking towards him. The woman, who was blonde, was pushing a pram. There was a young man walking beside her and the couple appeared to be arguing about something. It was nothing to do with Leonard, and he simply carried on looking for the cat. Then, almost without warning, Leonard found himself the subject of a brutal and unprovoked attack.

Leonard was punched and struck so that he sustained a fractured nose and bruises to his face. He also suffered a fractured ankle. The attack was over almost as soon as it had begun and, somehow, Leonard managed to get back to his house. Typical of his attitude, he didn't want any trouble and refused to involve the police – though he did tell his wife what had taken place.

Over the next week or so, Leonard recovered slowly from most of his injuries, though he did find it extremely difficult and painful to walk. Then, on Monday, 14 August, Leonard's health took a sudden turn for the worse. An ambulance had to be called and he was rushed to Noble's Hospital, arriving there at 5.30 p.m. It was all to no avail. Leonard Osborne was pronouced dead on arrival.

Details of the earlier attack were now passed on to the police. Furthermore, a postmortem, performed by Dr Bill Awler, a Home Office pathologist who flew to the island on Wednesday, 16 August, showed that Leonard had died as a direct result of the injuries he had sustained. A murder inquiry was now launched.

The inquiry was led by Detective Inspector Guy Pickard of the Serious Crime Unit. He issued a public appeal, printed in the island's newspapers, which read: 'We are trying to trace a man and a blonde woman, who may have had a baby in a small pram or pushchair, who were seen arguing in the lane at the time of the attack.' That appeal brought rapid results and, on Thursday, 17 August, sixteen-year-old Gavin William Patterson was taken in for questioning.

Patterson, who lived in Hillside Avenue, Douglas, was already well known to the police and had a string of previous convictions. On 16 July 1998, he had been given a probation order for common assault. This was followed by an offence of assault causing actual bodily harm, committed on 14 January 1999, for which he was given twenty-five hours' community service. He also had convictions for possession of drugs and criminal damage.

Patterson was asked to give details of his movements on the night of the attack, and was then released without charge, on Saturday, 19 August. Meanwhile, the police were checking out what Patterson had told them.

The blonde-haired woman seen with Patterson in the lane was his girlfriend, Kiely Regan. She told officers that she and Patterson had been at a party on the evening that Leonard Osborne was attacked. At one stage, they left the party to take their baby home and, as they passed down the lane behind Westbourne Drive, Mr Osborne had come around a corner, looking for his cat. For no apparent reason, Patterson had become angry with him and attacked him. But at no time did Leonard retaliate. Afterwards, Patterson had returned to the party and there he boasted to his friends that he had hit an old man.

Interviewed again, Patterson claimed that he could remember nothing of the incident. He was, nevertheless, charged with manslaughter, though he was released on bail. That led to yet another conviction and on 22 March 2001 Patterson was jailed for twenty-eight days for an additional assault.

Patterson made his court appearance on Monday, 26 November 2001, before Acting Deemster Carter. He was defended by Mr Anthony Berry, and the case for the prosecution was in the hands of Mr John Jones. Before the case came to court, Patterson had continued to deny any involvement in the death of Leonard Osborne, but now he changed his plea and admitted that he was guilty of manslaughter.

Evidence was still given that Leonard Osborne had died of a thromboembolism. He had started to suffer chest pains in the days after the attack, and his sudden inactivity afterwards, due to his fractured ankle, had caused an embolism in his blood. The actual cause of death was given as a thromboembolism.

For the defence, Mr Berry stated that Patterson had argued with his girlfriend and Mr Osborne had come upon a volatile man who was extremely disturbed at the time. Patterson had thought his girlfriend was about to take his baby away from him, though that did not, of course, he said, excuse such a violent and unprovoked attack. Mr Berry concluded that this was a ghastly event, but it had: '... brought home to him [Patterson] the terrible nature of the act he committed and he is jolly well going to have to do something about it. He is full of remorse.'

Deemster Carter accepted that Patterson had intended no serious harm and also took into account his guilty plea. Sentencing was adjourned until 10 December, for social inquiry reports, and on that date Patterson was sentenced to two and a half years in prison.

Understandably, Leonard Osborne's family were devastated. His wife, Shirley, told the press: 'We are disgusted with it. There is no fair sentence for a coward of this nature. The thing about this case is that this man has an armful of convictions involving violence, some of which were committed after he killed my husband. The law is ridiculous.'

These sentiments were echoed by other members of the immediate family. Leonard's son, William, said, 'The sentence was a joke. It was far too lenient.' Leonard's daughter, Jenny, and his sister, Evelyn Dougherty, also told reporters of the kind and considerate man they had now lost from their lives for ever.

In fact, it wasn't just the family who believed that the sentence handed down to Patterson had been far too lenient. In due course, the Attorney-General, Mr John Corlett, took the unusual step of entering an appeal himself. This was finally heard in July 2002, before Deemster Tattersall, where Mr Corlett stated that a more appropriate sentence was one of four years.

He went on to argue that Patterson had attacked someone much older than himself, without provocation, and then left the scene without bothering to check whether or not his victim was seriously injured. Finally, John Corlett cited the recent case of Bernard Aitken, who had received six and a half years for a similar type of offence. That sentence should have been the starting point in Patterson's case, he argued, and then reduced according to the circumstances.

The verdict, when it came, was that the sentence of two and a half years was the appropriate one and Patterson was sent back to prison to serve out the rest of his sentence.

The entire legal arguments on the sentencing had centred around the belief that Patterson was contrite, that he regretted his actions, that he had not intended to kill, and that he had learned his lesson and was now full of remorse. Some degree of that remorse may be seen in an event that took place in October 2004.

By then, Patterson had served most of his prison term and been released on licence, but in early October he appeared in court again, charged with affray. Apparently he had lashed out at passers-by during the TT races. He had hit out at a man on the promenade in Douglas, attacked another man who tried to intervene, and also two others who merely tried to tell him not to get 'worked up'. Patterson pleaded guilty to that affray and was sent back to prison to serve out the last three months of his sentence, together with a further three months for the affray.

It was not recorded as to whether he showed any further remorse on this occasion.

23

The Double Killer

At around 11.45 p.m. on Friday, 8 February 2002, police officers called in at Leece Lodge, a care home some 2 miles outside of Douglas. The Lodge was split into three separate houses numbered, unsurprisingly, Leece Lodge 1, 2 and 3.

In two of those lodges, 1 and 3, four young people and live-in staff resided. The other lodge, number 2, had just one occupant, 16-year-old Samantha Barton, who lived there largely unsupervised and was able to come and go as she pleased.

The police visit was in connection with various young people who had gone missing and it was decided to search Lodge 2 as it was well known that Samantha received many callers. To their horror, when they entered the premises, officers found Samantha dead. She had clearly been murdered, and there were signs that she had also been sexually assaulted.

The very next day, Saturday, 9 February, a man out walking near the Douglas to Peel railway line on the Cronk Grianagh estate saw something in a thicket of trees. Closer inspection revealed the body of 16-year-old George Green and it was clear that he too had suffered a violent death. Furthermore, there were links between the two crimes and, as a result, the police were now looking at a very rare event on the Isle of Man, a double murder.

Both of the young people involved in this tragedy had led very troubled lives. Samantha Linda Barton had been born in Dublin on 18 May 1985 to Rose Burnell and David Thomas. Not long afterwards, Samantha's parents had split up, leaving Samantha and her elder sister, Lyndsey, alone with Rose.

By 1986, the family had moved to Manchester and it was there, in 1988, when she was still only three, that Samantha first came to the attention of Social Services. She had, apparently, displayed temper tantrums when she was as young as eighteen months old, and now her mother asked that she be taken into voluntary care, along with her sister. Over the next few years the two girls were in and out of care a number of times, until they moved back to Ireland. Then, in 1992, when Samantha was seven, the three family members moved to the Isle of Man. Rose's sister, Theresa Barton, already lived on the island and it was thought that another family member's influence might calm matters down.

In June 1995, by which time she was ten, Samantha was sent to Knottfield, a residential care unit. The staff there soon found themselves unable to cope with her behaviour and she was duly sent to yet another home, Cummal Shee.

In February 1997, Samantha generated international headlines, though of course her name was not revealed at the time. On the tenth day of that month she had been arrested and held at Onchan police station charged with three cases of assault. The following month, an attempt was made to place her with foster parents, but that failed after just eight days. Soon after this, in June, Samantha answered the charges of assault and, since nowhere suitable could be found to place her, she spent two weeks in the Juvenile Justice wing of the Isle of Man prison. The fact that an 11-year-old girl had been sent to prison was flashed around the world. Luckily, in July, a place was found for her at St David's Alternative Support Centre in Pembrokeshire, Wales, and Samantha ended up spending sixteen months there.

In 1998 she was transferred to another unit in Gloucestershire, but her stay there was short lived and in November of that year she was sent back to the Isle of Man and Cummal Shee. The next month she was allowed to live with her aunt, Theresa, but she too was unable to control her and at one stage Samantha went missing for two weeks. Back before the authorities once again, Samantha was then sent to St Catherine's Centre for Girls, at St Helens on Merseyside, in February 1999. She returned to the Isle of Man two years later, in February 2001, when she lived within yet another care project at Maple Avenue. She stayed there for just one month before being moved to the Greeba holiday flats on Derby Road where she largely took care of herself. Finally, on 4 September 2001, she was sent to Leece Lodge 2 where she lived alone. The hope was that she would be given a degree of independence to prepare her for adult life.

Things were little better for George Green. He was born on 27 December 1985 to Margaret and Edric Green. George had three older sisters, but unfortunately the family also had a history of violence, aggression and alcohol misuse. On 16 January 1998, George was placed on the Child Protection Register, but he only really came to the attention of the police on 24 April 1999 when there was a major incident at his school, Ballakermeen School. George had been abusive and threatened a teacher there and, by May of that year, had been charged with actual bodily harm and attempted robbery. His mother refused to have him home and George, like Samantha, was sent to Cummal Shee.

In March 2000, George was transferred to Eden Grove, a unit in Cumbria; it was said that he appeared to be happy enough there. The problem, though, was that his family remained on the Isle of Man and visiting was difficult.

Towards the end of 2001 it was decided to allow George to return to the island for Christmas and, of course, his impending sixteenth birthday. The plan was that he would be temporarily transferred to a unit at Foxdale, would then be allowed to return to his family for a few days over Christmas, then back to Foxdale and, finally, back to Eden Grove on 7 January 2002.

There were problems from the outset. George was growing up now and wanted a degree of independence for himself. He flatly refused to go to the establishment at Foxdale and was then allowed to stay with his mother. He absconded from that address on 21 December and began to engage in criminal activity. He was arrested and remanded in custody from 30 December until 7 January 2002, and was released on condition that he caught the boat back to Cumbria. It was all to no avail and George ran away again in January.

Over the next month he was arrested a total of six times, but never charged with any offence. Each time he was bailed to his mother's address but, like Samantha, it seemed that it was impossible for anyone to control him. By the time the two youngsters died, in February 2002, Samantha had no less than sixty-four convictions for violence, drugs and dishonesty. George had forty-nine, for the same sort of offences.

The double murder probe was led by Detective Inspector Guy Pickard. There was, however, another investigation going on at the same time. On 17 November 2001, a group of four friends had gone on a camping trip in a lane adjacent to the Tromode Industrial Estate. The following day, one of the group, a 14-year-old girl, had told a friend that she had been subjected to a sexual attack by one of the two young men. This friend passed the information on to a social worker who in turn brought it to the attention of the police. As a result the 14-year-old was interviewed and, on 18 November, the alleged attacker was arrested. That man was Peter Charles Newbery.

There was, however, a number of problems. The 'victim' refused to make any official complaint. She also refused any forensic or internal examination, and Newbery himself denied that there had been any sexual contact. The investigation, though, was thorough and the young girl's clothing was sent away to the Forensic Science Laboratory at Chorley, for examination. It was not, unfortunately, marked for fast-track processing which meant that the results would take some time to come through. As a result, Newbery was released on police bail, until 20 February 2002, when it was believed the scientific results would be in.

On 12 January 2002, Thomas Draycott, one of the forensic scientists carrying out the examinations, reported back to the police in Douglas to say that he had found traces of Newbery's semen in the crutch area of the girl's jeans. This did not, however, prove that intercourse had taken place and there was insufficient evidence to re-arrest Newbery. That, if it happened, would have to wait until all the results were in.

Now, though, Newbery's name came to the attention of the detectives investigating the double murder and a check was made on his history and background. What the officers discovered made uneasy reading.

Newbery, too, had a long history of involvement with the police and the authorities. He had been convicted of an assault on 28 October 1996, and suspected of a burglary at Castleward Farm in April 1997. From 18 June 1997, he had been a resident of David Gray House, a residential establishment run by the Salvation Army. On 6 April 2000, he had been placed on probation for two years and, on 12 September of that same year, had served a prison sentence of thirty days. There was, though, another factor that rang alarm bells. Prior to all this, Newbery had also been at Cummal Shee, at the same time as Samantha Barton, and there had been rumours that, although he was only sixteen at the time, and Samantha was only twelve, there might have been some sort of sexual relationship between them. There was never any proof and no formal accusation was made. It was nothing more than a suggestion, but it may well have been the reason for moving Newbery from Cummal Shee.

Whatever the truth, Newbery had a long record of offending at the time of the murders and, of course, was under suspicion of having sexually attacked a 14-year-old girl. That, and other evidence, led to Newbery being arrested on 9 February 2002, the same day that George Green's body had been found. Soon afterwards, he was re-arrested on the sexual offence charge against the 14-year-old.

The trial of Peter Charles Newbery originally opened in

June 2003. However, Mr Ian Glen, for the defence, said that he needed more time to prepare his case and the proceedings were put back to July. The trial duly re-started but, at the end of the month, Acting Deemster Bromley-Davenport stated that he was unable to continue hearing the evidence. The jury were discharged and the court adjourned until 8 August, when a new trial date was due to be set.

Finally, in August, the new date was decided and Newbery was informed that he would face his trial in November. The proceedings finally opened on 10 November before acting Deemster Simon Fawcus. The case for the defence was led by Mr Ian Glen, assisted by Mr Paul O'Neill and Ms Louise Byrne. The case for the prosecution was led by Mr Tim Holmroyde, assisted by Ms Linda Watts.

The similarities between the two crimes were now outlined. Both Samantha and George had been strangled with shoelaces. George had been stabbed in the chest and Samantha too had been attacked with a knife. Details were also given of a pair of trainers found in a tree, close to George's body. These had belonged to George, and both shoelaces had been removed – suggesting that the laces found around the teenagers' throats had been taken from those trainers.

Witnesses were called who had seen Newbery at Leece Lodge 2 on the day Samantha was killed. A boy of sixteen (who had been just fourteen at the time) said that he had been standing at the door of Leece Lodge 1 at 2.30 p.m. on Friday, 8 February 2002. He saw Newbery coming out of Leece Lodge 2, but almost immediately Newbery went back inside and closed the door behind him. He then came out for a second time and locked the door behind him. Soon after this, the boy saw a note in the window of Samantha's lodge. It read 'Gone to court and to have a drink, back at 7 p.m.'. The inference was that Samantha was killed at some time before 2.30 p.m.

This fitted in with evidence given by some of the staff at Leece Lodge. They reported that, at 8 a.m., Samantha had been given a wake-up call, which she answered. At 8.15 a.m., some members of staff went into Leece Lodge 2 to talk to Samantha and they noticed a young man standing at the back entrance. At 11.15 a.m., Samantha had knocked on the front door of Lodge 1 and told the staff there that she and the young man were going to court and would be back later. This young man could not be identified as Newbery, and may well have been George Green. There was a suggestion that George and Samantha might, by now, have been boyfriend and girlfriend.

Newbery did give evidence on his own behalf. He claimed that he did know Samantha and George and had been their supplier of cannabis, ecstasy and speed. He also admitted that he had sex with Samantha, in a cemetery, on 7 February, the night before she had died. He denied having anything to do with the deaths of Samantha and George and claimed that they had probably been killed because of the theft of someone else's drugs.

The jury retired to consider their verdict on 15 December, after a trial lasting more than five weeks. They were out less than three hours before returning to court and announcing that Newbery was guilty as charged. The proceedings were then adjourned for a month before sentencing.

One week later, Newbery was back in court accused of the sexual assault of the 14-year-old. For the prosecution, Ms Watts asked that the matter be allowed to lie on the files and not be proceeded with. The defence agreed and the ruling was made.

In fact, Newbery was not sentenced on the double murder charge until February 2004 when he received a mandatory life term with the recommendation that he should serve a minimum of twenty years.

An appeal was entered, but dismissed on 30 September 2004. In the meantime, Newbery had been sent to a prison in the United Kingdom, to serve out his sentence. Soon after the appeal had been lost, an inquiry into the care of young people on the island was announced. It had come far too late for Samantha Barton and George Green.

24

A Web of Lies

In 1989, Jennifer Mary Barlow, who was aged just seven, moved from Garstang in Lancashire to the Isle of Man with her mother, Jane, and brother, Adam. Jane was divorced from her husband Stephen, who remained in England but she had now married again, her new husband being Leslie Griffiths.

Jennifer Barlow was a normal girl who loved horse riding. She and Adam attended Park Road Lower School before moving on to St Ninian's High School in Douglas, where she obtained good examination results, in 1998. From there, Jennifer briefly went to the Isle of Man College, but she soon became rather bored with her studies there and left. She took a job working in the New Look clothes shop in Strand Street and also worked as a barmaid at the Forrester's Arms. In addition, Jennifer was a member of the Army Cadet Corps.

Even before she left St Ninian's, Jennifer had met a young man one year older than she was: Thomas Christian Corlett. The two seemed to get on quite well together and even started dating. To begin with, though, their relationship was not a very serious one but, by August 2003, the couple were living together in Friary Park, Ballabeg, with Corlett earning a living as a freelance web designer.

On the morning of Sunday, 23 November 2003, Corlett's mother Lynn had called to visit the couple. But by 10 a.m., there were many other visitors at the house in Friary Park, because Jennifer lay dead in the bedroom and Corlett admitted that he was responsible, but claimed that it had all been a tragic accident.

On Monday, 24 November, Home Office pathologist Dr John Rutherford arrived on the island, together with a team of forensic experts from Chorley. The police investigation itself was led, at this time, by Detective Inspector Rob Kinrade, who interviewed Corlett after having arrested him on suspicion of murder. Corlett freely made a statement explaining how Jennifer's death had been an accident, but his story was not accepted and he was formally charged with murder that same day. The very next day, 25 November, he made his first appearance before the High Bailiff, Michael Moyle, and was remanded until 16 December.

The inquest on the dead woman opened on Friday, 5 December, before the deputy coroner, Mr Alastair Montgomerie. Evidence of identification was given by Jennifer's brother, Adam, who had viewed her body at Noble's Hospital on the Sunday. Adam had felt that it would be too distressing for his mother to make the identification as she had been badly affected when she had had to do the same when her second husband, Leslie Griffiths, had been killed in an accident in 1999.

Details of the cause of death had been given to the coroner by Dr Rutherford. Mr Mongomerie would only reveal the most basic details at this stage and confirmed that Jennifer had been killed by pressure applied to the neck. That same report had also mentioned a number of other factors in this case that would eventually be made public, and it was perhaps this that caused Mr Montgomerie to say to the family, 'My thoughts, and indeed those of many, are with you at this very difficult time and will be with you throughout the ordeal you will have to go through in relation to her death.'

Corlett made a number of appearances in court before finally being committed for trial. That trial opened on Monday, 17 January 2005, before Deemster Doyle. The prosecution case was detailed by Mr Tim Holroyde while Corlett's defence lay in the hands of Mr Stuart Lawson Rogers.

Asked how he wished to plead, Corlett replied that he

pleaded guilty to manslaughter. The prosecution rejected that plea and confirmed that they would proceed with the charge of wilful murder.

It had now been made clear than in addition to the strangulation itself, Jennifer Barlow had suffered other indignities. According to the prosecution she had, in effect, been tortured. Her hair had been shaved off; two of her teeth had been removed; and two obscenities had been tattooed on to her body. Corlett's defence would have to explain all these factors, but first the prosecution called witnesses to show that they had been part of a deliberate process of torture and abuse.

Dr Catherine Adams was a forensic dentist and she had examined Jennifer's mouth, and the two front teeth that had been removed, and which were subsequently found in the bedroom where Jennifer had died. Dr Adams stated that these teeth could have been knocked out by a blow to the face, or been extracted deliberately. Marks had been found on the adjoining teeth and Dr Adams explained that Jennifer's teeth overlapped those adjoining and a blow to the face might cause the teeth behind the missing ones to become chipped. Further, the roots of the teeth were unusually short and so would have come out more easily.

Dr Geoffrey Craig, an odontologist, had also examined this evidence but felt that the teeth had been forcibly removed. The damage to the other teeth and Jennifer's mouth itself indicated that a pair of bloodstained pliers, found in Corlett's room, had been used to remove the two teeth. Of course, the very fact that the pliers had been found suggested that they had been used on Jennifer.

Louis Molloy was a tattooist with twenty-three years' experience in the trade. He had examined two tattoos found on Jennifer's body. One was of the word 'Whore', which was in capitals, 4 inches long in total. The other was a swear word, 6 inches long, and also in capitals.

Both had been done with a needle by an amateur. The swear word was somewhat blurred and would have been done while

Jennifer was moving. The tattoo of the word 'Whore' was neater and, in Molloy's opinion, Jennifer would have been either compliant, unconscious or dead when it was done.

On the sixth day of the trial, Monday, 24 January, the time came for Corlett to give his version of events. He began by saying that on the evening of Saturday, 22 November 2003, he and Jennifer had been drinking in the kitchen. From there they moved to the bedroom where they played a football game on his Playstation. They had previously agreed that the loser would have to do a forfeit in the form of sexual favours.

Jennifer lost and, after some thought, Corlett had suggested that the forfeit should be that he would give her a skinhead haircut. She demurred but he badgered her and, after a time, she finally agreed and he shaved her head. They then stayed together in the bedroom for fifteen minutes or so and at one stage he told her that he still thought she looked 'Cute'.

After those fifteen minutes, Jennifer went to the bathroom and Corlett could only assume that she caught sight of herself in the mirror there, and did not approve of what he had done because when she came out she was screaming at him. She swiped out at him at one stage, but he managed to dodge her and, in reaction, he punched out, hitting her in the face, and she fell on to a coffee table. The inference here is that it was this blow that had caused the two teeth to come out.

At this point, Corlett had bent down over Jennifer to ask if she was all right but she came at him, threw herself upon, him and pinned him to the bed. She was shouting and screaming at him and lunged forward, trying to bite his face. Corlett managed to use what he described as a Russian martial arts move to grip Jennifer around the neck and jaw, and at the same time, was able to wriggle out from underneath her. She was now lying face down on the bed and he held her there with his legs, knees and one hand. He knew he had to restrain her somehow so, with his free hand, he reached out for the cord of his dressing-gown.

Taking the cord he looped it around her head and shoulders, but as they struggled he saw it ride up around her neck. He could do nothing and said, 'I locked up and froze. I knew what was happening but I just couldn't let go of the cord. I couldn't let go for love nor money.' Explaining what happened next, Corlett said, 'She went limp and slumped forwards in what seemed like seconds.' He continued, 'The thought flashed through my mind that she was dead but I thought – "No, give her the benefit of the doubt".'

Corlett now rolled Jennifer on to her back, and tried to find a pulse; he could not detect one. He snapped her necklace as he felt it might be restricting her airway and tried to bring her round by sitting her up in bed and moving her legs. During this process, she fell off the bed a number of times and he had to pick her up and put her back.

According to Corlett's continuing testimony, he now tried to wipe the blood from Jennifer's face with a flannel, but she just continued to bleed. In order to staunch this, Corlett then put a sock into Jennifer's mouth, a tissue in her ear, and cigarette butts up her nostrils, claiming that he believed the filter tips, being porous, would soak up the blood better. He then wrapped her face in a towel and cradled her to keep her warm. Finally, he went to sleep beside her and didn't wake again until his mother called on the Sunday morning.

There were still some points Corlett needed to explain. Jennifer's teeth and hair had been found in his wardrobe and the prosecution claimed that these had been kept as trophies. Corlett denied this. He had found the teeth on the floor after all this was over, he said, and had thrown them into the wardrobe in disgust. He had done the same with her hair while she was still alive, so that she would not get upset if she saw it.

Turning to the tattoos, Corlett admitted doing the swear word on Jennifer's back and said that, not surprisingly, she was not impressed. He had promised to cover it up for her with a large Egyptian symbol in a week or so. As for the word 'Whore', that was just his friendly nickname for her, he said.

Corlett claimed that he and Jennifer had had an open

relationship and had discussed marriage. He admitted the existence of Nimi, another woman he was seeing, and having sex with. According to Corlett, Jennifer had been fully aware of this relationship. Closing his evidence, Corlett said that on the day that Jennifer died, he had been drinking heavily. He had drunk around ten glasses of whisky with a dash of water and a few glasses of wine. Finally, Corlett stated, he was also suffering from Asperger's Syndrome.

The trial came to a conclusion on 25 January when, after a deliberation of two and a half hours, the jury announced that they had found Corlett guilty of murder. At a later hearing in March, he received his sentence for that murder: life imprisonment with a minimum term of eighteen years and eight months.

Only now could further information be published. Acting Deputy Chief Constable Gary Roberts, who had taken over from Detective Inspector Rob Kinrade in the early stages of the investigation, confirmed that Corlett's computer showed that he had visited some rather sick websites. More telling perhaps was a report published on 27 January, from an ex-girlfriend of Corlett's.

The woman, who remained anonymous, described Corlett as a 'manipulative fantasist' and a 'pathological liar'. The woman went on to say that she had been involved in a relationship with Corlett since October 2002 and it had lasted for some ten months. During their time together she had complained to the police three times about his behaviour.

When they first met, Corlett had told her that he was a dotcom millionaire and, even though she did not believe him, he persisted in saying that he was a wealthy man. It wasn't until she met his mother, Lynn, that she learned the truth about her new boyfriend – and he reacted to this revelation by smashing up his mother's kitchen.

After he had moved in with this woman, Corlett's behaviour had become more and more erratic. Once she had told him to leave and find somewhere else to sleep and the next morning she discovered that he had slept on her garage roof.

Some time later he came home drunk, asked her to play fight with him and, despite her protestations, she ended up with large welts on her arms.

The final straw came on her birthday when, during a barbecue, he smashed up his own music decks with a samurai sword. She threw him out, but for three weeks he bombarded her with text messages and telephone calls.

Still the case involving Corlett was not over. In March 2005, soon after Corlett had been sentenced, Jennifer Barlow's mother, Jane Rainey, made a plea that he should never be released. In fact, Jane would later, in July 2006, make one more appeal.

It was Tynwald Day at St John's and both Jane and her son Adam took up the ancient right to petition for redress of grievance. It had been revealed that Corlett was still at the Victoria Road prison on the island and the point had been made that it would be against his human rights to be moved from there. Jane quite properly pointed out that she and her son also had rights and they both continued to suffer, knowing that Jennifer's killer was still on the island. Jane Rainey's petition asked that Tynwald restore her 'right to freedom from oppression by removing the murderer from the Isle of Man prison to suitable incarceration in the United Kingdom'.

On 9 November of the same year that Jane Rainey made that petition, it was revealed that a prisoner found guilty of murder, but whose name could not be confirmed, had been told he would be transferred to a prison in the United Kingdom. The decision had been made in September, but the prisoner had been given time to respond to his transfer notice. Finally, in November, the notice was issued and the prisoner, widely accepted to be Thomas Christian Corlett, was informed that he would be moved off the island.

25

A Perfect Couple

Postman Kevin John Lindon and his wife Joanne Lee Lindon seemed to have the ideal relationship. They had been married for twelve years and had three children and appeared to be very happy together, but things would change towards the end of 2003.

It was at that time that Kevin had an affair with a fellow worker at the post office. The relationship developed rapidly and soon Kevin told Joanne what had happened and left his family to move back in with his father. At first, Joanne was devastated, but she was also a resilient woman and slowly she learned to cope. Indeed, she more than merely coped; she began actively to enjoy life again and develop a great deal of independence. She took the view that she simply needed to get on with her life.

Kevin's affair did not last very long and it was just a matter of weeks before he realized that he had made a grave mistake. He was certain now that he wanted to be back with Joanne. She was far less committed to the idea, and told her husband that she needed more time to think things through. She wasn't saying no to the suggestion – but, equally, she wasn't saying yes either. So for the time being, that was how things would remain: Kevin living at his father's house in Farmhill Gardens, while Joanne continued to live in the marital home at Hilltop View, which was about one hundred yards away.

Giving Joanne more time to think did not sit easily upon Kevin Lindon's shoulders, and eventually his mental health began to suffer. At the end of January 2004, he took an overdose of paracetamol, washed down with the best part of a bottle of whisky. Kevin had, however, been due to pick up his 3-year-old son from nursery school and, when he didn't show, a concerned Joanne went around to his home and found him. Kevin was rushed to Noble's Hospital where prompt medical attention saved his life.

As a result of that suicide attempt, Kevin was then admitted to the Ard Aalin psychiatric unit at the Ballamona Hospital, Braddan, where he spent a total of five days. It was clear, though, that he still had a good deal on his mind for, after being discharged, he drove his car up Marine Drive where he again contemplated suicide by jumping off the cliffs. The final sign that Kevin's mental problems were far from resolved occurred towards the third week of February when his father, John, found him lying in bed with a large knife underneath the covers.

Despite his problems, Kevin returned to work at the post office. Then, on Friday, 27 February 2004, while he was halfway through his delivery round in Farmhill he called into Joanne's house at Hilltop View, ostensibly to pick up a shirt that he had left there. Kevin did indeed pick up the shirt – but he also collected a bread knife from the kitchen.

Joanne Lindon was looking forward to that particular weekend. She had arranged to go on a trip to Chester with her sister, Alison, who lived in Lucerne Court, Little Switzerland. Kevin knew about this trip and, in his fragile mental state, grew more and more concerned over what would happen to his children while Joanne was away. That same Friday, Kevin made repeated telephone calls to Joanne's mobile phone, asking her who was to take care of the children. Though no one else was a party to what was said, Joanne was heard to say, at one stage, 'Don't threaten me, Kev' – implying that at least some of those calls were not of the friendliest nature.

After many calls, Joanne agreed to meet her husband to thrash out the matter. Kevin said that he would drive over to her sister's house in Lucerne Court and Joanne said she would come out to the car when he arrived, and speak to him. It wasn't very long before a final call told Joanne that Kevin was outside and waiting for her.

To be on the safe side, Ian Morrow, Alison's husband, went outside to check that everything would be fine. He saw no reason to suspect Kevin of anything untoward and went back into the house to tell Joanne that it seemed to be all right. Reassured, Joanne went outside and got into Kevin's car. It was then just before 9 p.m.

Within minutes, she had been stabbed a total of eleven times, the fatal wound being a 10-centimetre-deep wound to her neck. Kevin Lindon made no attempt to escape. He simply took out his mobile phone, dialled 999, and told the officer who answered, 'Hurry up, hurry. Just help her. I've stabbed her.'

Kevin Lindon faced his trial for murder on 13 June 2005 before acting Deemster Simon Fawcus and pleaded not guilty to murder, but guilty to manslaughter. Lindon was defended by Mr David Aubrey and Mr Jason Stanley, while the case for the prosecution was put by Ms Linda Watts. In all, the proceedings would last for three days.

Much was made of Lindon's own version of what had happened inside his car on the fateful evening. He claimed that he had only ever taken the bread knife from Joanne's kitchen with the intention of taking his own life. He had asked Joanne what would happen with the children while she was in Chester, and she implied that it was no concern of his, adding, 'You're not needed any more.' He had then taken out the bread knife in order to kill himself, but she had merely said, 'Do us all a favour.' Lindon had snapped at that point, lunged forward and, before he really knew what he was doing, stabbed his wife eleven times.

The verdict, when it came, was that Lindon was indeed guilty of manslaughter. Deemster Fawcus then turned to Lindon and, sentencing him to five years added, 'You have not only deprived your children of a mother, you have deprived them of a father and you have done incalculable harm to the surrounding family.' It was recommended that Lindon should serve at least two-thirds of his sentence. As the prisoner was led away, he turned to Joanne's family, who had been in court, and said, 'Sorry. I am sorry.' In reply, a voice from the public gallery shouted just one word: 'Liar!'

Joanne's family were far from satisfied with the result. Outside the court Lenny McCubbin, Joanne's father, told reporters: 'We are devastated and disgusted with the verdict. It makes a mockery of the legal system. We feel the jury acted reasonably on the evidence they were given. Unfortunately, a lot of evidence was not put to the jury.'

The case of Kevin Lindon was still far from over. An appeal against the leniency of the sentence was lodged by the attorney general, Mr John Corlett, and heard by Deemster Kerruish and the judge of appeal, Geoffrey Tattersall, in October of 2005.

At this hearing it was revealed that some one hundred and fifty letters had been received by the attorney general from members of the public, expressing outrage at the five-year sentence. For the defence, Mr David Aubrey said that these letters were based on a misconception. They had supported the prosecution view that the crime had been deliberate and premeditated, but the jury had accepted that Lindon had intended to take his own life and had not planned to kill his estranged wife.

The court adjourned to consider the legal arguments and judgement was only given at the end of the month. The judgement was that the sentence was not unduly lenient. Deemster Kerruish said, 'The sentence was within the appropriate range for the offence of manslaughter on the grounds of provocation. Any contention, or belief, that such sentence was lenient is founded on the prosecution case, which was not accepted by the jury.'

Kevin Lindon never did serve the recommended two-thirds of his five-year sentence. In fact, he served just eighteen months and was released on parole in early January 2007. It was stated at the time that he was now living in Onchan. The last word on the case was left to Joanne's father, Lenny McCubbin who said: 'We had hoped he would not get parole. We feel vulnerable that he has been released and will be living in the island.'

Index